Come home Charley Patton

Also by Ralph Lemon

Geography: art/race/exile (2000)
Tree: belief/culture/balance (2004)

RALPH LEMON

Come home Charley Patton

WESLEYAN UNIVERSITY PRESS

Middletown, Connecticut

Wesleyan University Press
Middletown CT 06459
www.wesleyan.edu/wespress

Printed in China
Designed by Rina Root, The Root Group NYC
Typeset in in ITC Stone Serif

Library of Congress Cataloging-in-Publication Data
Lemon, Ralph.
Come home Charley Patton / Ralph Lemon.
      p. cm.
ISBN 978-0-8195-7319-3 (cloth: alk. paper)
ISBN 978-0-8195-7321-6 (ebook)
1. Lemon, Ralph—Diaries. 2. Come home Charley Patton
(Choreographic work: Lemon) 3. African Americans—History.
4. Choreographers—United States—Biography.
5. African American dancers—Biography. I. Title.
GV1785.L385A3   2013
792.8'2092—dc23   2012033265

5 4 3 2 1

to my family

Come home Charley Patton

When the dream came
I held my breath
with my eyes closed
I went insane,
Like a smoke ring day
When the wind blows
Now I won't be back
til later on
If I do come back at all
But you know me
and I miss you now.

"On the Way Home," by Buffalo Springfield, was the first song I danced to drunk. It was 1969, I was fifteen. We'd have dance parties every weekend at St. John's Church, which was a block away from my high school. There was a local band that played there all the time, and they'd do covers of Buffalo Springfield. They'd also play Creedence Clearwater Revival stuff, and "Louie Louie" was a standard.

On this particular night, Thanksgiving weekend, I remember, there was an early snowstorm, and I was really, really drunk. I'd been drunk before but not this drunk. My friends and I would connive my older brother and his friends to buy us pints of Smirnoff's Lime Vodka. Begrudgingly, they would always do it, agreeing to the stupid and necessary truth of our passage. But this time before handing the pint over, my brother shook his head and said, "Y'all need to read James Baldwin." Who? "Baldwin, James Arthur Baldwin, who said, 'When I was growing up I had no writers, no artists—maybe a couple boxers.' Y'all need to think about that." What? Boxers? Chuckling, like little winter ducklings, how my friends and I sincerely and predictably responded. My brother also knew that Baldwin, whoever he was and whatever he represented, had no real meaning in this part of the passage.

I'd drink the whole pint, always, guzzling. One gulp. Then I would normally pass out. I'd finish the bottle and would get fifty yards from my house and pass out in the middle of our block's back alley. In the winter the landing was often soft but deadly; frostbite is no joke.

On this night I made it to the party. I was with two of my friends. Minneapolis is different now, but then there were five black people in the whole city. That's a joke, of course. Sort of. (In 1963 the Cincinnati, Ohio, Department of Agriculture transferred 32 black families from Cincinnati to Minneapolis. Before that transfer the entire population of black people in Minnesota was at 2 percent. My family began the black migration of Minneapolis. "We made the city black," my father likes to say.)

The party was a sanctuary for many of my white friends, two of my black friends, and me, dancing . . . or stumbling around drunk to early Neil Young.

Though we rush ahead
to save our time
We are only what we feel
And I love you,
Can you feel it now.

And then Jeff Gunderson showed up. Jeff Gunderson was the city's best fighter—best white fighter. He would go to different parties in the different neighborhoods, neighborhoods of mostly white high schools. (The mostly black high schools were in a far different part of town, were mythological, were said to have governments and armies.) Gunderson would invade these parties to pick fights and kick the shit out of people. So he had a kind of tough-ass badge. And it was interesting because he was white, and he was really tough, fearless. Handsome, but he was missing teeth, a grinning absence that was part of his badge.

Obviously, my two friends and I were easy targets, walking into this party. So Gunderson sent his friend up to me, and his friend said, "Jeff has picked you guys to fight tonight." I was eighty-five pounds, ninety max. I was also teetering from side to side, while trying to comprehend his challenge. Jeff was a giant and his friend was a smaller giant, and I was drunk. The guy said, "I'll fight you, and Jeff wants to fight your big black friend over there." My big black friend was Grover. Grover could fight, but he was crazy. He didn't evaluate situations well, and this was not a good situation. "So talk it over with your friend, and I'll come back at the band's next break to set it up, cool," Gunderson's friend said and then walked away. So Grover wanted to do it, but I told him I thought it wasn't really a good idea. Grover, we're really drunk, I said. There's a snowstorm outside, and Jeff Gunderson has picked us to fight!

The band took a break, and Gunderson's friend came back and said, "So, what do you think? Let's do it; we'll do it outside, right behind the church. We'll give you guys five minutes." I took the five minutes and cornered Grover and my other friend and announced, I'm going home. So I left, snuck out a side door. I ran all the way home, about two miles, alone in a snowstorm, cold, terrified, stumbling, in a lot of fresh deepening snow that was also moving all around me, being blown about by all the wind.

The following Monday, in school, I went to the library and began reading James Baldwin. But only one book, the only one there, *Go Tell It on the Mountain*, half-way, and then stopped. (Told my friends I thought *The Red Pony* by Steinbeck was far more plausible).

ONE IS NOT WATCHING EITHER TENDERNESS OR LOVE,
AND ONE IS CERTAINLY NOT WATCHING THE COMPLEX
AND CONSUMING PASSION WHICH LEADS TO LIFE OR DEATH
— ONE IS WATCHING A TIMOROUS AND VULGAR
MISREPRESENTATION OF THESE THINGS.

RETURNING FROM THE FAIR / REVENANT DE LA FOIRE

Thanksgiving, Thirty-Four Years Later
November 20, 2000
Dear R,
About Thanksgiving, I feel a little homesick . . .
Also, I am a little sick that these grand people of America of great beliefs are giving thanks to God for all he has given during the year, only offer poor turkey. I tried, after reading your email to think of comparative African holidays. But I don't have to look at the entire Cote D'Ivoire for a like celebration. Right at my village, the village Ki-Yi, we had a celebration, December 19, where we stop to give thanks, pray, and present offerings of fruits and flowers and invite everyone to come share food, dance at this important occasion giving God thanks for all his blessing. Here, to stop and give thanks, the U.S. kills a turkey. Maybe I don't understand. Can you explain this to me?
Djédjé

November 22, 2000
Dear Djédjé,
I dunno, America, my home, is kind of an angry place. I just read about a tiny town in Utah, a town called Virgin, which enacted an ordinance requiring a gun and ammunition in every home, for self-defense. The mentally ill, convicted felons, conscientious objectors, and people who cannot afford to own a gun are exempt. Weird, right? And we talk a lot of trash in this country. Maybe we live here and are homesick too and don't know it. This is some of what I heard on a few of the streets near where I live just the other day:

"When I kill yo' ass, don't tell me you didn't push me!"

"Will you please shut the fuck up!"

"My bitch is like a cigarette."

"That's my son, damnit! I love that little shit. Hell, I was his father for the first two years of his life."

"Yes, baby, OK, OK. I did call you stupid, I admit it, but I didn't call you crazy. I swear."

"Yo girl! I didn't just show some attitude. I was bleeding."

And I heard this on TV just last week:

"This music [jazz] don't have a damn thing to do with Africa."
—Art Blakey

Funny and sad, right?
Bye
R

One Hundred and Twenty Years Earlier (before life was funny and sad at the same time)
November 1866
This was nothing out of the ordinary. Abundant forearms, bulging, folding below deep-hued satins, swelling at the seams. Pews filled with large, shining faces crowned in wide-brimmed hats of Easter colors but it's not Easter. Nodding, sweating eyes barely open and drifting. And dark, mostly blue dresses with small flowers and fake necklaces that glow. The singing is deafening, and when it subsides there is talking exultation like trumpets hugging their wide, wide necks. Thick soft smoke under the seats, or maybe clouds.

Hearing the euphoria from the Mt. Zion AME Methodist Church, lying in his half-filled tub, Billy Belk said, "Them niggers act like God is hard a' hearing." From the other room a gentle voice responded, "No, honey, them folks just love Jesus, that's all."

I don't ever remember hearing his name, Billy Belk—Papa's father, not Papa. Papa's name was Frank Lafayette Belk.

It was Papa who I remember, who I had seen. My grandaunt, Aunt Mattie, gave me his pocket watch when he died. A thin gold Elgin with a gold chain. It was later stolen from my apartment in New York (along with a black leather jacket, a blue shirt, a pair of white high-top three-stripes Adidas, some underwear, and a new pair of Levis; the thief, who must have been around my same size, left his own ragged and soiled clothes behind, along with a dank chemical smell that stayed in my apartment for a week). Papa was not white, but he would pass for white when it was necessary. Papa was a barber. And I remember watching one of his daughters washing his white and thinning hair with a bar of Ivory soap. Papa sat in a chair next to his kitchen sink wearing a white, starched shirt and suspenders. I never saw Papa cutting hair. He wore a Panama straw hat and had wire-rimmed glasses. All of his daughters looked white. Six of them. Two also wore glasses. Birda, my mother's mother, "Mama Bill," second to the oldest in her family, would also pass for white when it was convenient. "I'll let 'em serve a nigger and not know it," she would say to herself, smiling, while sitting at a Woolworth's lunch counter having a sandwich. And there were times she chose to be black. Like the time she was taking my mother to an all-black boarding school, Mather Academy, in Camden, South Carolina (It was a school run by the New England Southern Conference of the Women's Home Missionary Society of the Methodist Church. All white teachers, pretty much. There may have been two black teachers.) My mother, who was high-yellow, in Lancaster County skin-color terminology, was around thirteen or fourteen at the time. They were on a Greyhound Bus and were both sitting in the front, where Mama Bill chose to sit. The bus driver told my mother that she would have to move to the back of the bus, my mother being "a shade or two darker" than Mama Bill. Mama Bill told the bus driver that my mother was her daughter and that she would stay put. The bus driver told Mama Bill that she could go and sit in the back with my mother, but that my mother could not sit up front with her. Mama Bill told the bus driver to stop the bus "and let us off this damn Greyhound!!" The bus driver left them off in Kershaw, South Carolina. Fortunately, Papa's half-sister, Aunt Beatrice, lived in Kershaw, and she called them a cab and they went on to Camden, Mather Academy.

Birda was named after her mother, Birda Belk. Birda Belk was more white than Papa, a full-blood German, no black blood whatsoever. But Papa was white enough, would walk ahead of his daughters while walking down the main street of Lancaster, South Carolina, he being more white. There simply was not enough space on the same sidewalk, he'd say. Fifty years later my mother held my hand as we walked down that same sidewalk to the movie theater and up the stairs to the balcony, where five or six other black people were. I don't remember the movie. Papa was a Methodist and went to church down the road from his house. His wife, Birda Belk, was Catholic. She went to a Catholic church in Chester. Catholics weren't too accepted in the South in those days, so every Sunday she would to go to church a few miles away in the town where she grew up.

Billy Belk, Papa's father, was taking a bath at the end of the day. A tall, bony, dark man. The tub was small, his knees bent high and tight. And barely enough water to cover his genitals. She had just finished washing his back. Then he fell asleep. And when he woke up, he was blind. "Mattie, I can't see no more," he said, naked and wet.
Had gone blind. That's the way the story has been passed down.

February 1999
Dear Anita,
I dreamed last night that I was dancing with Papa Satterwhite. It was the second time. He had a wide-legged step, low to the ground and rhythmic. I danced alongside him, and here's the strange part, I was invisible. Interesting, right? It got me thinking . . . I need you to get some information for me, from Mom, about Papa's father, Mom's great-grandfather, the one who went blind.
1. What was his name?
2. Was he tall? I remember being told that he was tall.
3. Was he dark-skinned or light? Somehow I imagine him pitch black.
4. What was the name of his wife? What did she look like?
5. Finally, how did he actually become blind? If known.
I would appreciate as many answers as you can gather. Write them down exactly as Mom answers. Please.
Thanks.
Love
R

Dear Ralph,
Papa's father was William (Billy) Belk, which is why they called Mama Bill, "Bill." As a little girl she used to lead him around when he was blind. She loved him tremendously.
I called Aunt Mattie and she said that he was of average height, looked to be five-foot-eight to five-foot-nine. Kind of round but not fat. He was a quadroon (white father, mulatto mother). He had several wives, three to be exact (all of color). Papa's mother was wife number two. After she passed, Billy Belk married another light-skinned woman. How he became blind, she didn't know. She thinks he might have had glaucoma.

We have a picture of Papa's mother, Mattie Mcdowell Belk. Aunt Mattie was named after her. She said she has a picture of Billy Belk holding Papa when he was a baby. She's sending it to me today. The super-old picture Mom has of Papa when he was a young boy, he was posing with Billy Belk and his third wife, and Papa's half-sisters. AL

Mama Bill's name was Birda Belk Satterwhite. She was named after her mother, Papa's wife, Birda Belk. Her sister Mattie, named after Papa's mother, named her daughter Birda Rose. The Satterwhite name came from my grandfather, W.I. Satterwhite. Everyone called him by his first two initials, "W.I." William Isom, grandson of Isom Caleb Clinton (on his mother's side), a slave to a white lawyer named Ervin Clinton, who disobeyed South Carolina law by teaching the brightest of his slaves to read and write. Isom Caleb later became a bishop, and his brother, Frederick Albert, also born into slavery, became a state Republican senator of Lancaster County during Reconstruction. W.I.'s father, John William Satterwhite was a pharmacist. His father was Edward Satterwhite (a mulatto); mother, Lucinda Gary (mulatto). Edward's father was John Satterwhite (caucasian, a Revolutionary War officer and hero from Virginia).

I was five years old the first time I saw W.I. His large body was resting, folded in a metal wash-tub, bathing in his tiny kitchen. The same sparkling tub he would drink from on his porch on the weekends.

William Isom Satterwhite was tall and (red) black. A carved large-boned face. He was mostly bald, but bald like a magnified boy after a fresh haircut, not bald like a middle-aged man losing his hair. Road-map eyes, grinning with his large handsome body as though drinking were nothing more than an excited game of cards. W.I. sat on his porch with his youngest son, Trent, the two of them surrounding a metal washtub filled with orange juice, moonshine, and ice.

The day before, I sat on his lap on the same porch and eagerly watched him peel radishes. Fresh from his garden. He said that I would like them. I tried. They burned, I spit them out, and he nodded and smiled.

That summer of '57: climbing and then standing on a high horizontal branch, then pulling my pants down and peeing down through the labyrinth of green leaves and branches, aiming for an opening that gave way to a dusted splash down onto the red dirt road. "Country rain," that's what the older, larger boy had called it. That's how he demonstrated. But with such aplomb, climbing the tree, higher, so fast, and then making it rain like a deluge. His penis was the biggest thing I had ever seen, bigger than my father's. He also taught me how to smoke a cigar, in the same tree. Our backs propped up, resting, high up on the narrowing trunk. Sitting, legs long on lower branches. I got dizzy and fell, far down, with no aim. Soft bones bouncing in the colorful red dust.

On a much later summer eve W.I. was too drunk for the porch, his son, and family, and ran through the woods because he believed that if he didn't run the big bright-colored animals chasing him would trample his body and eat his flesh. After that incident my mother never saw him alive again.

"Mama would send us away on the weekends because he only got drunk on the weekends. She didn't want us to see him drunk, not the way he got drunk. During the rest of the week he was a good father. Would kill a white man if he had to, if his family was threatened. Fearless. W.I. played trumpet, in a troubadour band, the Lancaster Midnight Serenaders. They would practice in the front yard. The thirties, forties. He knew W.E.B. Du Bois. Du Bois would come to the house to talk to W.I. It was the beginnings of the NAACP. W.I. was a very smart man. Generous to a fault. Owned a lot of land but would get drunk and gradually signed it all away to his friends. My poor daddy."

Dear Anita,
More questions for Mom:
When did W.I. die? The month and year? How old was he when he died? And when did our family visit him for the first time? I remember we took the Greyhound bus. I had to sleep on the bus floor because there were so many bodies crowded in the back. Was W.I. a member of the NAACP? Why and when did W.E.B. Du Bois visit him? Also, what was the date of Mama Bill's death? How old was she when she died?
Thanks.
Love R

Ralphie, are you there? I'm on the phone with Mom as I email you. Here are the answers:
1. W.I. died from a cerebral hemorrhage, February 21, 1961.
2. He was fifty-five years old when he died.
3. That first family trip south, to Lancaster, was in July 1957.
4. Yes, W.I. was a member of the NAACP along with John Jacob Clinton (Uncle Bub, W.I.'s uncle).
5. W.E.B Du Bois came to visit Uncle Bub, the only black doctor in Lancaster, to set up a chapter of the NAACP in Lancaster. They had their first meeting in the AME church. Mom doesn't know what year that was. She does remember meeting Mr. Du Bois at Uncle Bub's house. She's not quite sure how old she was, but she says she had to have been around nine or ten years old because it was before she went to Mather Academy and after Mama Clinton died. (She was eight when Mama Clinton died.) So she puts it around nine or ten. You choose.
6. Mama Bill died April 21, 1991.
7. She was eighty-four years old. She had just turned eighty-four on April 12. She was born in 1907.
8. W.I. was born in 1905.

That's it. Any more questions, let me know. Mom is going to Lancaster tomorrow to see after Aunt Mattie. She's got to have angioplasty. (She has some blood clots.) But it's outpatient so she'll be home, if you want to call her (803-285-5807). She'd love to hear from you. Her surgery is Friday, March 12th.
Love to you
AL

April 21, 1991
Mama Bill lay in a rented hospital bed in her youngest daughter's house in Minneapolis, Minnesota, far from Lancaster, South Carolina, watching the only light in the room, professional wrestling on a twelve-inch television screen at two o'clock in the morning, eyes glazed but a huge grinning mouth, almost gaping, and her nightgown soaked. Cheering.

Eight years later her sister Mattie went to the hospital, March 21, 1999. On April 7 she was still in the hospital, rehabilitating, had lost most of the movement on the left side of her body. A mini stroke. She was heartbroken.

"Spends most of the day crying. She was doing so well. You know she's eighty-five years old. She was so proud and active. I don't think she'll recover from this," my mother says.

The last sister. So my mother treats her like she's the last family matriarch. An era. Her childhood. One of the final opportunities for my mother to reconcile the complete possibilities of being a mother. Mattie understands the same tradition. The tradition will not recover from this. (My mother has three daughters. One daughter who will only be a mother once. And two daughters who will never be mothers. At some time they were taught that happiness does not depend on parturition.)

April 14, 1999
Hello, Aunt Mattie?
"Yesss."
Hi, it's Ralphie boy. How are you?
"Hi, sweetie."
I've been calling all over the place for you.
"Oh, I'm fine. I came home on Tuesday. I'm doing better now but still a little weak so I'm taking it easy. Watching television, and maybe walk around the house a little, that's all."
Well be patient, there's no hurry, no place you have to run off to.
"Yesss, yesss . . ."

There is something about how the women of Lancaster say "yes," have said "yes." Drawn out to a three-second meter, hypnotic.
Her voice was soothing. A kindness beyond anything I have known since I had last spoke to her, since Mama Bill's funeral, I think. I promised that I would visit her soon. She told me that she would look forward to my promise, my visit, in a tone that seductively demanded I not let her down.

Routing a Reconciliation
June 20, 1999
Wow, I didn't know he had done drugs, I say, sitting in the back seat of my sister's white Toyota Corolla, taking notes. (This is research after all.)

"Yeah, he was a congressman, you know, along with Andrew and all of them other politicians."

When did this happen?

"Oh, way back in the eighties. Messin' with that young singer. Lost his congressional seat. Cocaine. They probably set him up. You know white folks."

"Have you been to your brother Mike's new house?" My mother abruptly shifts, asks.
"Yes, he has, don't you remember? He was there for Mama Bill's funeral," my sister answers, driving.
"'91, that's right. And it'll be another nine years before he's down there again."

I hope that's not true.

Mama Bill was eighty-four. "She had Lupus but also her heart just wore out. I think it was really the medication they had her on—Prednisone. Seems like yesterday, but that was long ago. Yeah, Aunt Mattie's all that's left of the sisters."

And, as abruptly, the subject changes from death to architecture. My mother and sister enjoy driving through upscale walled communities where imagined houses look alike and there's not too much space between them.

I'm not fond of driving through upscale walled communities and change the subject. You know, I've started re-reading James Baldwin. What an interesting voice right now, oddly not at all reductive . . . not as much as I would have thought.

"Who?" My mother mumbles.

James Baldwin, I say. And change the subject again.

Mom, what did you want to be when you were in college, before you left school, ran off with Dad and got married, moving to Cincinnati?

"I wanted to be in theater, to act. But my daddy said it wasn't time. I was in all the plays at school. I easily memorized all my parts and everybody else's. My daddy said it wasn't possible for me to act then, said the time was not right. He was a musician, played the trumpet and had to play for white folks, so he knew. Living in the South made my daddy the way he was. He was a smart man but couldn't get anywhere. My daddy used to love Louis Armstrong.

"If I had stayed down there I'm sure it would have been bad. Once my mother sent me to the store with a note for groceries. The owner was an old white man. He filled the order and put whatever change was left inside the bag of groceries. And as I turned around to leave, he lifted up my dress and patted me on my butt, put his hands down my panties. Mama never sent me there again, told me not to tell daddy 'cause he would have surely killed that old man, and that would have been so much trouble. I was no more than seven."

The car comes to a stoplight. We take a left on Lawyers Road to Mint Hill where we take a right, Highway 51. At Idlewild, we take a left, to 485 South (the Interstate part of the outer belt).
"Don't they have an Idlewild Airport up in New York?"
No, not that I know of.
To South 521 off 485.

Pass Indiankind. We are no longer in North Carolina.

"Lancaster County used to be Lancasterville. Same white folks who settled up in Pennsylvania. They settled up there first."

Forty years ago blacks converged on "Back Street" in downtown Lancaster, South Carolina. The whites governed from Main Street. "Back Street" is now White Street, a little Southern American post-apartheid humor. Main Street is now abandoned.

We park at the old house. 113 Pleasant Hill Street.

My mother looks up at the big house in disrepair. "The big house had first and second floor porches that wrapped around the house, the first double-decked wrap-around porches in the whole city. We kids used to play and even sleep on the porches, listening to music coming from the Masonic Hall across the street. That's where they say Louis Armstrong played when he came to town, before he was famous." The porches had been removed years ago. To be more precise, they had fallen off. The Masonic Hall still stands and is currently being used by a church group.

William greets us, "Hi ya get along, hi ya get along."

William used to be Mama Bill's boyfriend; now he keeps Aunt Mattie company three days out of the week. Trent, my mother's older brother, also drops by.

Trent is an aging Southern cowboy, of sorts, the horseless kind. Inevitably, after about twenty minutes, the subject of guns comes up, Lancaster's particular Castle Doctrine.

"I like to go out back and shoot my gun in the air," Mattie says.

Sounds dangerous, I say. Don't you worry about where the bullets might fall?

"No, I never think about that, I just enjoy shooting. And it makes so much noise. I likes that."

"William, didn't you give Mama a little bitty gun that she kept in a drawer in her bedroom?" my mother asks.

"Yes m'am, tiny, you could put it in your shirt pocket, a 22."

"That ain't no gun," Trent joins in.

Trent knows guns. Has a gun tucked away in every room of his house. Sometimes more than one. Planted in creative places behind sofas, on windowsills, and in empty flower vases. He swears he has a working bazooka hidden away but no one present has ever seen it.

"Trent was so drunk he asked his sons, Billy and Little Trent, to hold him up while he was turkey shooting. And he won the biggest turkey at that turkey shoot, brought it home, drunk still. Like Lee Marvin in *Cat Ballou*," Mattie recalls.

Everyone laughs.

"Yeah, I told my boys to carry me over there to the target. I asked them if there was any dust on the target. They said, 'No, Daddy.' So then I told them to 'hold me up while I shoot at that damn turkey.' I shot my gun and they both screamed, 'Daddy, you hit the bulls-eye!'"

Everyone laughs.

"Hell yes, here's how it's done. When shooting at somethin' aim an inch lower than the target cause the kick will always send the barrel up an inch and right where you're aiming."

William nods, concurring. William also has an interior cache of guns decoratively placed throughout his house, garage, and 1982 Cadillac.

But there's only one little bitty gun at 113 Pleasant Hill Street. The big house, Frank Lafayette "Papa" Belk's house, built in 1860 by Papa's father, Billy Belk, where he one day went blind in the tub, where Birda Rose now lives. Birda Rose inhabits one bedroom, bathroom, and the kitchen; the rest of the house is closed off. Birda Rose is Mattie's daughter. Mattie grew up in the big house, was born there, so was Birda Rose, so was my mother, and her mother.
Mattie now lives right next door in 113 1/2 Pleasant Hill Street. A small house built in the fifties. Inside it smells sour and sweet, with no furnishing older than the seventies. The "older stuff" is locked away in the big house, on the second floor where neither Birda Rose nor anyone else ever ventures. "That part of the house is dangerous 'cause it's too big and too empty," Mattie says.

"Too big and too empty," Birda Rose sighs. There is no man in Birda Rose's house. There used to be, "but he died of a heart attack in church. Now in Lancaster all the black men are in prison so if you want to find a man that's where you got to go. Meet them there, through church programs or something like that, and then wait till they get out."
That's where Birda Rose's daughter, Bridgette found her husband. Bridgette seems happy with the results. They also live fifty miles away from Lancaster.
Mattie Mcdowell Belk was married once, to a "pitch black" man named Andrew Jackson, Birda Rose's father, who's still fancifully alive, "a lady's man at eighty-nine." Mattie never passed for white but she could have.

When I was a teenager, Mattie would send me money on my birthday, addressed to "Master Ralph Lemon." Mattie continues to fill envelopes with new ten-dollar bills for the boy children, "chaps," who she's partial to on their birthdays. Those close enough to her to still run through her house, but not the girls, as if the girls didn't need the new ten-dollar bills. It is a tradition. She writes the boys' names, addresses, and dates on the envelopes, all of it illegible. This visit, she hands them to me and then asks if the spellings are correct, addressed to the right great-grandson, distant cousins who I've never met, who are complete strangers to me. I'm supposed to pass them out, when the right great-grandson arrives, today, the next day, the day after.

Mattie regularly receives floral shop "special occasion bouquets," potted flowers, from family and friends, which she replants outside around her house and then forgets to water. On this particular morning my mother is up early, outdoors watering the forgotten flowers, those that haven't died.

Mattie has three meals a day. For breakfast: Oat Bran or Cheerios with fresh bananas or canned peaches. Dinner: green beans and grilled chicken breast. Before bed she has graham crackers with milk and fresh or canned peaches.

When I first came to Lancaster in 1956, I remember the peach tree in the backyard of 113 Pleasant Hill, that and the chickens. The peach tree and chickens are gone. The countryside now filled with paved streets and shotgun houses, all with porches.

Earlier in the day we'd taken Mattie to Applebee's. She was at first reluctant, hadn't been out to eat in years, she confessed. At Applebee's we ordered for her: French onion soup, grilled chicken breast, steamed vegetables, and sweet tea. She seemed to enjoy herself. But later, back in her living room, confessed, "I won't be going out again, no, not with my teeth movin' aroun', makin' so much noise as I try to chew, embarrassin'. No, I won't do that again."

Mattie turns on the television. "Ruth, you like the stories?" she asks my mother. Mattie watches *The Days of Our Lives, The Guiding Light.* "They do some terrible things on these shows, terrible! But I likes to watch 'em, I do."

Mattie's house is full of photographs, on walls, framed, and propped on almost every table in the house, and there are piles of photo albums. Photos of family members, mostly copies, of her father, Papa, and her sisters, Francine and Irma. And then there are lots of photos of grandchildren and great-grandchildren. Most of the old photographs are of her father, Papa, Frank Lafayette Belk. Small ones, big ones, framed, unframed.

"Papa would drink now. A little beer. Never in front of us though. He also smoked. He kept two beers and some ice in the wood house and in the chicken house. He'd go out there by himself and have a smoke, take a sip, never finishing a whole cigarette or beer all at once."
Mattie pauses, remembers something, sits with her hands folded in her lap, then blurts out, "I forgot to tell y'all, I just now had my pistol fixed, on Wednesday, and it came back so shiny!"

There is something about being in the South that is heartbreaking. I discover that this is not just a family matter.

An Incomplete Chronology

1863 Emancipation Proclamation
1865 Thirteenth Amendment formally abolishes slavery.
1933 Arne Bontemp's *A Summer Tragedy* is published.
1938 Blues artist Robert Johnson dies of poisoning in Three Forks, Mississippi.
1947 Under President Truman the phrase "civil rights" moves into common political parlance replacing the phrase "the Negro question."
1948 Gandhi is assassinated in Delhi, India. I am born in 1952.
1953 James Baldwin's *Go Tell It on the Mountain* is published.
1954 Supreme Court outlaws school segregation in *Brown v. Board of Education*.
1955 Fourteen-year-old Emmett Till is lynched in Money, Mississippi, for reportedly flirting with a white woman in a small-town grocery store. I take my first bus ride south in 1956.
1957 Congress passes first civil rights act since reconstruction.
1957 Jill Johnston, dance and art critic, writes her third critical essay on dance, titled "Abstractions in Dance."
1958 Merce Cunningham premieres *Summerspace*, music by Morton Feldman, set by Robert Rauschenberg.
1959 Bob Dylan moves to Minneapolis from Hibbing, Minnesota.
1960 Robert Dunn begins a composition course at the Cunningham Studio.
1961 Simone Forti makes *Huddle*, a community body-based work.
1961 Freedom Bus Rides begins, testing a recent Supreme Court ruling for the desegregation of interstate travel through the South.
1962 First Concert of Dance by the Judson Dance Theater.
1963 June. Medgar Evers, NAACP director in Mississippi, is shot and killed in his driveway in Jackson.

1963 August. March on Washington. Martin Luther King's "I Have a Dream" speech.
1963 September. Four teenage girls die in a church bombing at Sixteenth Street Baptist Church in Birmingham, Alabama.
1963 Nina Simone reaches No. 2 on the UK charts with a song from the hippie musical *Hair*, "Ain't Got No/I Got Life."
1964 Lucinda Childs makes her *Carnation* solo. Steve Paxton creates solo *Flat*, Bruce Nauman has first performance of *Wall-Floor Positions*, and president LBJ signs Civil Rights Act of 1964.
1964 Also Freedom Summer. The voters' registration drive in the South. Chaney, Goodman, Schwerner brutally murdered in Philadelphia, Mississippi.
1965 Trisha Brown makes *Homemade*, a solo with a camera on her back. In July Congress passes Voting Rights Act.
1966 Yvonne Rainer makes the seminal *Trio A*.
1966 (Little-known) Ben Chester White, who had worked most of his life as caretaker on a plantation, who had no involvement in civil rights work, is murdered by Klansman who thought they could divert attention from a civil rights march by killing a random black man.
1968 March. Merce Cunningham premieres *Rainforest*, music by David Tudor, silver clouds by Andy Warhol.
1968 April. Martin Luther King is assassinated in Memphis, Tennessee, while working with the embattled sanitation workers' strike.
1972 Steve Paxton instigates Contact Improvisation.
1975 I attend my first dance class with Nancy Hauser at the Guild of Performing Arts in Minneapolis, Minnesota.
1976 My daughter, Chelsea, is born.

January 2001

I travel to Cincinnati, Ohio, to take pictures of the place where I was born. The whole time I am thinking about the American South, well aware that Cincinnati is not the South, but across the Ohio River is.

February 2001

I travel to Sapelo Island, Georgia, to discover something authentic about the American South. "We are not Americans," they tell me. "We are Sapeloans." I discover that Sapelo Island is too far south (for my purposes; and in the ocean). I also discover boneyards there, whole trees falling where they stand, due to beach erosion, becoming skeletal. And I hear rumors of an existing Ring Shout dance called the Buzzard Lope tucked away in some old Geechee man's body. A very interesting place and also very abstract.

May 2001

My daughter and I reenact the Freedom Bus Ride of 1961. Thirteen original Riders, seven black and six white people, including John Lewis, left Washington DC for New Orleans on two buses, a Trailways bus and a Greyhound bus, and traveled through the South testing a recent Supreme Court ruling on the desegregation of interstate travel, the stations' waiting rooms, restrooms, and restaurants. Our reenactment marks the fortieth anniversary. This research turns out not to be too far south, and not too abstract, and in fact, sits perfectly in the middle, geographically and in time. So it seems.

Overview

After a Chinese dinner on May 3, 2001, keeping to the historical map and research itinerary whenever possible, we left Washington DC for our first stop, Richmond, Virginia, arriving on May 4.

After a couple days in Richmond visiting friends and sightseeing, we took another bus to Danville, Virginia, the first place the original Riders were refused integrated service. From Danville to Charlotte, North Carolina, where there occurred the first arrest of one of the Riders due to, of all things, a shoeshine.

To Rock Hill, South Carolina, site of the first incident of physical violence. A mob of twenty attacked the group, and John Lewis was the first to be hit as he approached the white waiting room.

From Rock Hill to Atlanta, Georgia, where the Riders met with Martin Luther King on Mother's Day (and my daughter and I spent four days with my family).

From Atlanta to Anniston, Alabama, where forty years ago the Klan was waiting and one of the buses was fire-bombed. The group took another bus and continued the rides. Another group on another bus arrived in Anniston and were also brutally attacked.

To Birmingham where the first group of Riders was replaced because of the violence at Anniston. And another group of ten was arrested in Birmingham and spent the night in jail. They were literally driven out of town by police chief "Bull" O'Connor, who left the group stranded on the Tennessee border.

To Montgomery. Ah, Montgomery. Where, according to John Lewis: "Out of nowhere, from every direction, came people. White people. Men, women and children. Dozens of them. Hundreds of them. Out of alleys, out of side streets, around the corners of office buildings, they emerged from everywhere, all at once, as if they'd been let out of a gate. To this day, I don't know where all those people came from."

Where John Lewis almost died. Where James Zwerg, a young white man, was beaten and never attempted to defend himself, even as his face was stomped into the ground. "Kill the nigger-loving son of a bitch!" They sang.

To Jackson, Mississippi, where over the next several months wave after wave of Riders were eventually marched off to Parchman Penitentiary, three hundred in total.

From Jackson my daughter and I continued to New Orleans, the original final destination of the Riders, where I bought a used trumpet before flying home, a Bach.

Throughout our modern and air-conditioned bus ride, we made side trips: to Greensboro, North Carolina, site of the cataclysmic Woolworth's sit-in of 1960, "the first sit-in," and to Durham, North Carolina, where there was an important but little publicized sit-in in 1957. There were side trips to visit family in North Carolina, South Carolina, and Georgia.

A side trip to Selma, Alabama, to ritually walk the Edmund Pettus Bridge, site of "Bloody Sunday," the beginning of a seminal civil rights march in 1965.

We had ritually structured events in all the mapped Greyhound bus stations and in the spot where the Greyhound bus stopped, burning on Route 21, outside Anniston, Alabama. At Kelly Ingram Park, in the rain, scene of protesting children, police dogs, and fire hoses of 1963. And the Sixteenth Street Baptist Church in Birmingham. I bowed in the driveway of 2332 Margaret Walker Alexander Drive in Jackson where Medgar Evers was assasinated.

I found confused and fleeting ways to make my presence known in these highly charged spaces that are not the same spaces of forty years ago. That have elusive memories. But the civil rights movement did happen. There are photographs and books. Taxi drivers, white and black, are useful historians, "Where did this happen, where did that happen? Hell, I don't think I remember." "This used to be a thriving black neighborhood, commercial area." Or "This was Klan country, all back in the hills there, where everyone seemed to be named Adams."
Now, many of the Interstate motels, Days Inns, gas stations in Georgia, Alabama, and Mississippi are owned and operated by Indian émigrés.

Alabama is scenically one of the most beautiful places I've traveled.

Every event or structured activity was documented in order to contain the immediate moments. Capturing evidence that these personal events/actions did happen, and with some specificity. These events were not designed for an audience, at least not a conventional audience. The self-consciousness of these private acts created a radical pedestrian quality. Hyperinconspicuous. I did not want to disrupt the communal ecology of these spaces. There were, however, installations created in all of our motel rooms for the very certain audience of housekeepers. I left stamped American-flag postcards for them to respond, with a promise to pay them fifty dollars if they did. I only heard back from one motel, from an Indian émigré housekeeper, named Neal.

Throughout the trip Chelsea made sure we ate at least twice a day. And most strangers assumed that she was my sister, my girlfriend, or maybe my wife.

Routing a Reconciliation II (Retracing the Freedom Bus Rides)
May 3, 2001
Chelsea and I take a train from New York City's Grand Central Station to Washington DC's Union Station. We find a Chinese restaurant and have dinner, like in the original script. A different Chinese restaurant, of course.

The next day we meet with my distant aunt, Joan, for breakfast. Joan is Mattie's sister Carol's daughter, and my mother's cousin. She introduces us to Lawrence Guyot. Lawrence doesn't drive and doesn't have a computer. Walks to work. Has been a Catholic and civil rights activist all his life. He's from Mississippi.

"Most human beings in this country are way too complicated to predict unless they are from Mississippi, deep South, where the people are either really evil or really good." Lawrence, a very big man, holds court, picking at a tiny salad, for two hours in the Holiday Inn's dining room. Softly ranting, biblically, about the civil rights movement, how its beginning courage came from the Scriptures, a specific faith. That the great despair that was black society in the South and throughout America was spiritually muted because black society generally had faith.
(I thought how curious that the rage of that despair, the impossible despair and rage of white racist terrorism, did not itself turn to terrorism. Unless one can claim terrorism of the self as another kind of violent metamorphism. And here, it might be important to question the modern American black temperament and how it has been shaped by what could be historicized as insidious rage exhaustion. Baldwinesque, "It's taking too long," he would always say. I didn't share any of this thinking with Guyot, and he didn't mention James Baldwin in his long list of civil rights–era heroes.)

Lawrence Guyot gives us a list of his relatives, ones we should contact once we've reached Mississippi, "really good people."

Chelsea and I take a taxi to the Greyhound Bus station right behind Union Station and not far from the Holiday Inn, an eight-dollar ride by taxi. Everywhere close by costs eight dollars in DC. DC is not really the South, not really. And in the South "people are more stupid," the taxi driver says, after I complain about the eight-dollar fare for such a short distance.

The young employees of this Greyhound Bus station are friendly. The bus station itself is narrow with many separate lines of (walled-in) waiting passengers. It has an indoor Hardee's. No counter to sit-in, only standing hamburger orders, shakes, fries, etc. There are benches on either end of the station.

There are many of us going to Richmond and many buses leaving for Richmond. The line is long. Eventually, if you started in the back of the line, waiting, you'd be in the front of the line, waiting, because buses come and go often enough, leaving irate would-be passengers behind until they're in front of the line an hour later. And then they get a seat, any seat they want.

The bus to Richmond is full, with mostly black people. Except one Asian woman, one male Asian Buddhist robed monk, a tall, young white Marine, a fifty-something hatless cowboy (wearing a brown plaid short-sleeved shirt, tight white jeans, slightly belled, black cowboy boots, greased-back hair and holstered cell phone). And two young white girls with babies, white babies.

The white driver is considerate, asking if the air conditioner is working in the back of the bus. It isn't. It isn't working in the front of the bus either.

The ride takes two-and-a-half hours. Bearable. The two babies cry for an hour and forty-five minutes. The Marine sleeps, snoring. The cowboy sleeps, snoring. The many other black riders supply the harmony.

I don't see much out the bus window. Instead, anticipating all that is to come, I close my eyes and listen to the extra radio noise coming out of the earphones of my daughter's Walkman, worn backwards, which creates a better sound for her, she says.

At our first stop in Virginia I was confronted with what the Southern white has called "separate but equal." A modern rest station with gleaming counters and picture windows was labeled "White," and a small wooden shack beside it was tagged "Colored." The colored waiting room was filthy, in need of repair, and overcrowded. When we entered the white waiting room Frank Hunt was promptly but courteously, in the Southern manner, asked to leave. Because I am a fair-skinned Negro I was waited upon. I walked back to the bus through the cool night trembling and perspiring. —Freedom Rider William Mahoney

Oh, shit! We completely bypassed Fredericksburg, the Riders first test stop, fifty miles outside DC, where nothing happened. I had originally written it down as the first stop, but when I printed out my itinerary it was printed on the bottom of the page preceding the itinerary list, a page of random notes. I didn't discover this until a month later, at the end of the trip. For a moment, I thought we might have to start over, but only for a moment.

The gateway. The Richmond bus station is sprawling, with waiting passengers queued up along the four walls, the center becoming a vast open space. There are benches on either end of the station. The young employees here are not friendly, not at all. And they are more present than those in DC, more of them. The dress code is blue, long-sleeved for the drivers. T-shirts emblazoned with dogs for those hosting the ticket counters. The less official others, waiting for something in particular, things I don't see, like lifting luggage or repairing engines, they wear insignia polo shirts. All these indeterminate others are young black men.

And speaking of insignias and indeterminate others, in the two days we are in Richmond I am reminded of how black people continued to practice being Americans after slavery:
The Knights of Pythias
Lily Black Organization
The Friends Freedmans' Association and the Good Idea Council
The Vocational Ethic of Early Black Leadership:
    Teachers must love their work
    Students must love their work
    Students must love their teachers

I learn more about slavery:
    Rice slaves
    Cane slaves
    Cotton slaves
    Tobacco slaves
    House slaves
    Urban factory slaves
    At least those.

I am reminded that there was a "trolley boycott." That of course preceded the city's buses' boycott in the sixties. And there was "Beauty Culture," black entrepreneurism and products to whiten skin and straighten hair. That "American black culture began immediately, instantaneously," whatever that means.

In old Richmond, dance halls were always right above funeral parlors. These were not juke joints. And men were not allowed to grope women in these places.

I receive this information and more from a small homemade museum, the Black History and Cultural Center of Virginia, with photo remnants, recreation installations, and objects taped to the walls. From our museum guide I learn that black people talk differently about black history when a white person is present. The voice is more patient. Anecdotes take more time. And that black adult guides talk differently about black history to black children then they do to their parents. "It's hard for children to pay attention to history lectures."

I learn something of the Black Bourgeoisie, a blackness I know very little about. "White bourgeois families ask what boat you came on, black bourgeois families ask what church you belong to. Heard of the Cotillion? There's also the Botillion." A young black man from Hampton College, who works at the museum, admitted to being part of the black elite.

"I'm not supposed to tell anyone what my family does."

What do they do?

"My dad's a dentist and my mother is an English professor."

Oh.

I brush up on Second Street. The good life, until the times of the civil rights movement, which was devastating to the community, to many similar black communities in the South, to a fostered, vital, and guarded life segregated from white society.

"In Virginia black people made General Motors even more rich because they didn't want to sit in the back of the bus," a reverend tells us.

"Hello, Reverend." A man wearing a brown suit and thick horn-rimmed glasses enters the conversation.

"Hello, Bishop, how are you today?"

"Well, well. Had some excellent fish at Crockers. Do I smell like fried fish, Reverend?"

"No, no, not at all, Bishop."

How many cars, Reverend? I interrupt.

"I don't know. A lot of them though, Fords."

We have white friends in Richmond who offer to drive us to the bus station. It is our last day. On the way we detour and they show us the granite and marble parade of white men with swords and beards on horses, Monument Avenue, to the very end, where I'm told by a heavy-set middle-aged black man I look like Arthur Ashe, when he was alive, before he got sick. At the end of this stone parade the monument of Ashe seems out of place, no sword, no beard, no horse, and it's smaller than the rest.

Danville, Virginia, was the last Confederate capital. Now known for its many churches, more churches per square mile than any other city in Virginia. The bus station in Danville is tiny. A compact matrix of gray plastic places to sit. And a back room with a desk and a television. There's no place to have one's shoes shined.

A joyful, fat ticket agent stands behind the ticket counter, jeweled and wearing a little makeup, a new man of the South.

"You're not supposed to be in this room." Where the tiny TV is broadcasting a basketball game with the volume turned off.

Can I watch from outside?

"Yeah, that's OK."

A group of high school military cadets are dressing in the men's room. From T-shirts and jeans to gray and white and brass, full military dress. The ticket agent observes them as they enter and exit the men's room, his gold tooth glistening as he smiles. Yes, he is also watching a basketball game, when not unloading luggage and trading jokes with those newly arriving and departing.

From the Danville station we taxi to the Motel 8 on Riverside Drive. In the lobby is a young black male, a desk clerk, raising his voice at a middle-age white woman about the motel policy.

"We get reservations and we make reservations. We'll get you a double when one is available. Basic motel business, m'am."

"Well," she says, "it didn't used to be like that!"

"I'm not sure what 'didn't used to be like that' means, m'am. Sorry. Next in line, please." Which happens to be us.

I overhear him later in the lobby talking to a few women friends, who might also be family. His mood is much less edgy.

"You'd be engaged if you could cook," one of the women councils.

"I can cook. But I ain't engaged," he responds. "Everyone I been cooking for is married." He laughs.

"Oh, you better be careful. You could be kilt cookin' that way," the oldest of the women chimes in.

On the porch of a halfway house called Harbour House, we interview a group of substance rehabbers about living in the South and Greensboro, North Carolina, our next stop.

"Stay away from Martin Luther King Drive and English Street. Otherwise Greensboro is good."

"No, all of Greensboro is mean," an older man says.

What, it's violent there?

"Yeah."

"Danville used to be mean," says a man wearing a Minnesota Twins baseball cap.

What do you mean?

"I'm sitting on this porch in Danville minding my own business, that's what I mean. Those black folk on Martin Luther King Jr. Drive and English Street ain't got no sense, no idea how it's their own neighborhood that they is keeping down. Fuck anger, niggers! It ain't nothing but trouble. With anger you lose. And that music they listen to don't help. That's what I would tell 'em, if I was there, but I ain't, thank God!"

One of the rehabbers is a musician named Sonny.

"I got a band. I'm in a band, play guitar, we tour a lot. Taking time off, the band has time off. So I'm down here cleaning out. Too many drugs. Our CD will be out soon, so I'm cleaning out before we go on tour again, so I'll be ready. I didn't learn to play the guitar on drugs so I figure I don't need them now. You know, I lived in New York City for a while so this is a great meeting, happy to meet you."

Nice to meet you too, Sonny. Good luck!

The youngest rehabber talks about Mississippi, what he has heard about it, never having been there.

"In Mississippi white fathers had their white sons plant oak trees in their backyards, keeping the tradition, passing on the tradition."

James, the only white man at Harbour House is a young man from Lynchburg, Virginia, and is not sure how the name Lynchburg is related to lynching, if it is at all. "I have no idea," he says.

"How old are you?" the youngest one asks me.

I didn't answer and it really didn't seem to matter. No one reacted to my silence.

But then, "You asked me that same question, an hour ago," Sonny says to the youngest one. "Well, I have to spend time with you, maybe I'll have to ask you for money sometime, figure it will be good to know a little something about the person I'm asking for money." Everyone laughs.

The youngest one tells me he's from New York City. Lived in the Bronx, worked at Youngworld, a children's clothing store.

Where's that?

"I don't remember, near Forty-Second Street, I think. It was a long time ago." He doesn't seem old enough for it to have been a long time ago.

Forty-Second Street has changed quite a lot, is a different place, I say.

"Well, I know the Bronx is still one big project; that's all it is, still. I know that. Brooklyn, Queens, Bronx, Manhattan—all projects, if you ask me."

Not all, I say. Not anymore.

But I know what he means. At the moment these gentlemen seem to have very little in life, other than their recovery. A loss of what was mean, violent, and resistant. They have their empirical evidence. They are being taken care of, sitting on this quiet porch, seem wide-awake, and can think and say what they want. An obfuscation of sorts. And at this point I distract myself into another dreamy revelation . . . my fake questions, a coded message, an affirmation really, for full-blown racial injustice or integration as I see it, and my confusion with what to do with this modern-past inequality and faux-freedom, what I witness, right here, better to create concepts that I can play with, ideas mythical, empowered, distracted . . . like flying back to Africa with wings, real ones that sprout from the shoulder blades . . . back to Africa where I could start a rock band and play a trumpet like a guitar.
"Wake up, niggers!" says the man wearing the Minnesota Twins baseball cap.

Back at the Danville bus depot the fancy and jolly ticket agent is just starting his shift while a woman with giant glasses behind the ticket counter counts money to hand over to the company cash collector, a short plump white man with silver hair, red skin, casually dressed, with a pistol in his back pocket posing as a wallet. Meanwhile, a young Italian man, who doesn't speak English and looks absolutely terrified, sits and waits five hours to board a bus to Silver Springs, Maryland.

Downtown Greensboro, North Carolina

Before renovations the seventy-five-year-old Woolworth building, landmark of the first publicized civil rights sit-in, which will soon have a protected glassed-in restaurant-counter area and wax sitting figures, before there is a Hall of Civil Rights Leaders with their robotic animations, before the soon-to-be hologram exhibit of interviews with sit-in participants, and before all these architectonic plans come to pass, there is a spacious and noble bygone cafeteria, an art deco ghost with twirling red seats and simply open space and a dark, dank, and pristine basement stretching a whole block with an escalator frozen upward into faded golden sunlight.

At the Durham, North Carolina, public library I search for a sit-in that predated the "first" sit-in in Greensboro. A librarian helps me find a box of microfilm, under "segregation," dated 1957–58. I find a story about a sit-in at an ice cream parlor in 1958, three years before the '61 Woolworth sit-in. I make copies.

The librarian says, "Oh, I want a copy too. I had no idea. I'm gonna laminate it for my nieces, for their bedroom walls. Young people need to know their history!"

Excuse me, m'am.

"Yes?"

Is this a dangerous place, for your nieces? I ask, thinking about what the older man at Harbour House had said about Greensboro.

"No, not a bad place."

Are you sure?

"Well, pretty sure. I live here. But compared to someplace else . . . ? I don't travel much."

Bus Driver (with a short afro fade): "Travel much?"

Punk (with a pink and blond Mohawk): "I been to South Carolina, Georgia, Mississippi, Alabama, Tennessee, New Orleans, Florida."

Bus Driver: "Been to Arkansas?"

Punk: "No, ain't thought about Arkansas."

Bus Driver: "Been to DC?"

Punk: "Nope, never been that far north."

Bus Driver: "I been to DC. DC ain't nothin'. The White House is in the ghetto."

Punk: "Really?"

Bus Driver: "Yeah, crackheads, heroin, burglars, drag queens."

Punk: "Drag queens?"

Bus Driver: "Yeah."

Punk: "Right out front the White House?"

Bus Driver: "No, only to one side. Crack heads, heroin, muggers. The other side of the White House is good."

Punk: "Drag queens are ridiculous-lookin'. I went to a gay bar once and saw a drag queen there and had to leave. They look ridiculous!"

That was a conversation between the black male bus driver and a young white teenage girl sitting in the front of the bus, right next to him, dressed like a gutter punk, with pink hair, on the way to Charlotte from Greensboro.

This was a conversation between a mother and child on the same bus:

Child: "Waahhhh!"

Mother: "Stop screamin' child, use your inside voice!"

Child: "Waahhhh!"

Nigger Story I
My older brother, Michael, who lives in Charlotte, picks us up at the bus station and drives us back to his house. On the way I ask if he knows or has heard that Greensboro is a "mean" place. He said he didn't think so. Ever been called a nigger there? I ask. No, he says. So when was the first time you heard the word "nigger"? I ask him. I was with him when it happened, he says, when we lived in Minneapolis, 1963. Actually I was the one called "nigger," by a little white boy, whose name was Billy. My brother tells me this story once every couple of years, and I don't really mind. I don't remember the incident.

A mob of twenty young hoods with chains, sticks, and crowbars attacked the group, and John Lewis was the first to be hit as he approached the white waiting room.

From Charlotte we changed states, to South Carolina. The Rockhill bus station could be the same one of forty years ago. There are still pinball machines. Now the station is also a Laundromat. So we do laundry.

Today there's a big softball tournament in Rockhill. The Days Inn is full. Seemingly hundreds of muscular white men in permanently dusty uniforms roaming around with their wives and children. The families lean over railings, balconies, peering predator-like down toward the parking lot, looking at cars and at each other. The men play horseshoes first, in the Inn's picnic area, shirtless, before they head off to some park, in full uniform. The wives and children sit at picnic tables, watching, before heading off with their men to a park where they'll sit on bleachers, watching.

My first trips to the South were in 1957 and 1961, to Lancaster, South Carolina, not far from Charlotte. On the first trip my mother took my brother, two sisters, and me to meet our grandparents. We rode a Greyhound bus. I remember that the bus was full and I had to sleep on the floor way in the back, peacefully, under my mother's protective legs. I remember White and Colored drinking fountains and sitting in the balcony of a movie theater in downtown Lancaster. On the second trip the whole family drove down from Cincinnati in a '58 Chevy, for W.I.'s funeral. I mostly remember the thick fog in the narrow mountain roads of Tennessee, and watching my father sweating as he drove.

May 12, 2001
Lancaster, South Carolina. Another side trip.
Mattie Mcdowell Belk wore her "ear bobs" for our visit, a special day. A promise kept.
My uncle Trent also seems fit but later confesses to having gout. He says he has my grandfather's trumpet packed away in his attic. My mother hinted that this might be true, said that my grandmother got the trumpet out of the pawn shop shortly after my grandfather died.

Trent, could I borrow the trumpet for a couple years?

"Borrow it? I'd shoot you before I'd let you have it."

Trent decides he doesn't want to talk about the trumpet anymore, and begins to talk about Minnesota, where my family and I used to live. "My next-door neighbors are from Minnesota. They asked if they could have some salad from my garden, my collards, turnips. I said sure, just pick them out anytime you want. I even made them a little entry into the garden, a gate through my fence. They came in and ate the collards straight raw, wouldn't even wash them. My God, never seen that before," he says.

For a time when my family lived in Minnesota, my mother worked at a supermarket. She said that Minnesotans would toss away the greens of turnips. She would save them and bring them home for dinner.

William Isom, W.I., Trent's father, my mother's father, got an award every year for his gardens. "Victory Gardens" of World War II, that's what they were called. He'd work in the garden every evening. At the time everyone in town would grow his or her own food. The government would provide the seed.

Suddenly Trent is reminded of something else he has to do, another appointment. We say our goodbyes. "Trent ain't got no trumpet," Mattie says, as soon as Trent walks out her back door. "Next time I see him I'll ask, but I don't believe he's got it no more. That trumpet's long gone."

Mattie keeps the conversation flowing, telling us she had cataracts a few years back, before the angioplasty, and how she had heard that marijuana could help her distress. She convinced and paid a neighborhood thug to acquire some pot for her. The thug arrived with the pot, lit up, and then blew the dreamy clouds into her face. That was the arrangement.

Mother's Day with Martin

I've been to Atlanta, Georgia, where my parents and my immediate family now reside so many times that it's not like the South to me. My father's family is from Georgia, although my father grew up in Ohio. Still, I've heard the same rich "songs of the South" from my mother and father a million times. Stories they have partly made up.

On this trip I ask my father about the forties again, a period in time that interests me, when Black Internationalism began to fall apart for the first time. He remembered his time in the military in 1944, Fort Hood, Indiana. He was waiting for training orders to Fort Bragg in North Carolina. In the meantime he was ordered to pick up garbage around the base, along with all the other black troops. Interned German POWs had the easier jobs of overseeing the black troops and driving the garbage trucks. My father was outraged. "Working for the Nazis? Hell no! And anyway, there was no way they were going to know about my whereabouts with all the young black inductees working menially here and there, too many of us. So I hid out in the attic of the barracks for three days until I got my orders to Fort Bragg." I had heard this story only twice before.

He tells this one for the first time:

When Jackie Robinson played at Crosley Field in Cincinnati in the summer of 1947, black people came from places as far away as Kentucky, West Virginia, Tennessee, and Indiana, bringing lunch boxes of chicken and chocolate. The whites around us shouted, "Where is he, which one is he?" The only black player on the field.

Neither my father nor my mother have ever mentioned Martin Luther King Jr. in any of their memory plays. This does not surprise me.

After Atlanta the situation heated up.

Suddenly there is a green thicker than that of the Georgia pines, and there are mountains, small ones. It has been said that Alabama was mostly Klan country because it was mostly blue collar. Mississippi racism was more political, the White Citizens' Council, a white-collar and more elaborate racism. Georgia had the Klan and the original King family, whatever color collar that was. The political fashions of the South are now anybody's guess.

On the bus a man named Mohammed wearing a brown suit and bow tie shares a bean pie with some of the passengers. And then sells some. He has a large box full of them.

Anniston, Alabama. The bus station, not the same one of forty years ago, has been here for many years. Pristine and empty.

Anniston is quiet, depressed, and the white people wave at the black people. We share a taxi with a young black man who was on our bus from Atlanta. He is now off to a prison in Talla-haga for a nine-month reform program for drug trafficking. Been in trouble since he was nine-teen, will be twenty-four on June twenty-fourth. In a fatherly voice the taxi driver tells him how to handle himself at Tallahaga, says he knows it well enough.

The same taxi driver on another day gives me the scoop on modern-day Anniston: "Monsanto!

A big lawsuit. Everybody in Anniston has cancer from the plant. PCB, maybe, but not sure."

So, this used to be Klan country? I ask.

"All the Klan lived on the west side of Anniston and seemed like they were all named Adams, a whole side of town named Adams, seemed like."

Later I walk around our motel complex at dusk, run into a small group of white college students, boys, wearing baseball caps, oversized T-shirts, and baggy jeans, standing next to two SUVs. I walk past and there is a sudden sound of someone moving; the gravel around them crackles and I jump and turn around facing them. Everyone laughs.

"Yo, where you from, dude?" one of them asks.

Yo, New York, I answer. And pick up a piece of gravel.

"Nice baseball team sometimes, dude." He quips.

I walk back to the motel faster than I had come, tossing the piece of gravel into the air.

Tuesday, the next day, we eat sushi in downtown Anniston. The sushi chef is a young Mexican woman named Anna. The Japanese owner, Suki, is from Hawaii. Her restaurant has been open in air-poisoned Anniston for six months. Times have changed. Thank you and good luck, the food was lovely, I say to Suki, tipping Anna and grabbing a toothpick as we exit the restaurant. The fish was obviously not great, Anniston having toxic air and being landlocked, the fish frozen and all. Still I felt the need to be supportive. This is a long way from Hawaii.

After lunch we go on a search for the old Greyhound bus station, maybe the most infamous one. We find a taxi and encounter many variations on the location. More than a few black folks along the way are certain they know where it is, remember where it was, where it ends up not being. A barbershop around the corner from the old station turns out to be our best bet. The owner walks us through an alley to a small, yellow brick building, now a glass company. The taxi driver nods, yes, this is it.

From the station the bus sped out of town forty years ago with pickups and cars in hot pursuit. For years there was an abandoned gas station marking the spot where the bus exploded, was bottle-bombed outside Anniston. "A gas station owned by an Adams." The gas station is gone. Now, at this date, the spot is under construction, nimble earth movers excavating an expansion of Alabama Highway 202. Just a few months ago it was a single two-lane road. Not much room at all for the violent motored rodeo of forty years ago.

Anniston is co-joined to Oxford. I walk the Main Street of small-town Oxford and feel safer, not having a destination. White people in cars and black people in cars pass me by and don't look twice if they look at all—the odd pedestrian, I must appear. I don't see many strollers.

Outback Steak House in Oxford sits on a hill and overlooks the town, and if you eat there you will see no black people eating there. I don't. I've been in public environs like this before, where I'm the only person of color, but never before in Alabama, this far south. Here it is emotional and foreign. Chelsea and I eat with eyes wandering wildly through the restaurant the whole time.

That night and the next I have nightmares about Alabama: grotesque marching maps and white men blocking my way inside of cramped rooms. But no screaming, everybody's mute. Then a dream with Nina Simone singing "Ain't got no . . . ," a soundtrack to the earth movers obliterating the site of the famous bus-burning.

A white woman of the new South in a knick-knack store in Anniston said she remembers the Klan, those Adam boys, burning a cross across the street from her family home, how terrified she was. Her father told her "Those people are crazy," and moved the family north, to Atlanta. She's back in Anniston. "When I drive into Atlanta now I cry, I miss it so. I love it there."

Scenery. The bus rides begin to fade in distinction . . . and then we are in Birmingham.

I'm not sure I'm allowed in the basement. I go anyway and try to discern one stained glass window from another, none of them shattered. I photograph all of them and imagine that I know what I am looking for.

The Sixteenth Street Baptist Church on a Sunday in May is mostly empty. Mostly women of various ages with theatrical hats, colorfully spotting the sanctuary. A children's choir. And Mary Hope, a retired school teacher up North who came back home, Birmingham black royalty, whose grandfather helped settle Birmingham. Her family originally had 400 acres or so. Now she has a 150-acre tree farm. A tree farm and the church. She tells us the church is looking for a new pastor.

"Be careful about references, references can be tricky. You can call another congregation and they'll tell you he's great, because they want to get rid of him! That's why they'll say he's great. Be careful with references."

Sounds reasonable, I say.

She refers us to downtown Birmingham where there's a music festival, Cityscapes. Tickets to the event cost twenty dollars for the day. Early in the evening there's a middle-aged white blues musician who plays the blues like really good white musicians play the blues, deceptively and with the same excited, technically brilliant aggression with which they rule the world. Although Jimi Hendrix also played the blues that way.

Later in the evening thousands of young people, mostly white, fill the streets, cheering wildly, waiting for Nelly. The handful of black youth here who can afford the twenty dollars practice fraternity step-dancing, circled, barking, in a tiny obscure clump on the edge of the larger crowd; their big-butt girlfriends join in and so does one very drunk, fat white boy. The horde of other white boys and girls smoke cigarettes and look suspiciously, not at the small group of black kids, but at life.

Nelly is eventually rained out. Everyone goes home, the handful of blacks to their neighborhoods, the horde of whites to theirs. As I walk back to the hotel a car drives by and a black youth sticks his head out of the car's passenger's window and screams, "Faggot!"

Kelly Ingram Park. No dogs, no cops, no hoses.

It's still raining. I stand under a tree, sheltered for a long time, and discreetly videotape a teenage girl with an umbrella dipping it in and out of the park's fountain. And I observe the community of derelicts congregated under the band shell. A drunk comes up to me: "Listen, I'm no criminal and I don't want my picture taken, I mean it!"

Yes, I believe you. He follows after me for a block or so, watching, stumbling, making sure I don't videotape his trance. It stops raining.

A day later, we are waiting for the bus to Montgomery.

We meet Ruben Hector, another jailbird, burglary, just released and going home to Mobile. I give him twenty dollars to tell a story of how the prison system only gave him forty-three dollars for his entire rehabilitation. He tells the story and then takes my twenty dollars and immediately goes on a search nearby the station to buy sex. He almost misses the bus.

The Original Queen Cab Company drops us off and there are two small boys on bikes waiting in front of the Rosa Parks Museum, which is closed. I ask if they've been inside the museum. They nod—silent—and wait for the next question. It is slow in coming. And then never comes. We all wait. The downtown traffic is also silent. It must be another Sunday. I finally break the ice, our impending future, and say, "OK, thanks, goodbye." We walk off, waving. They get off their bikes, sit on the curb, and wait some more.

After visiting the Hank Williams Museum, which was open and not far from the Rosa Parks Museum, we call the Original Queen Cab Company again. This time we're picked up by another old black man like before, neither of whom were in Montgomery for the bus boycott. One was a soldier at the time, stationed at a base outside Montgomery in case there were riots during the boycott. The other driver, Franklin, was in New York "staying out of trouble."

Franklin has hip-hop playing on his car radio. I ask if he is listening to it, if he likes it. He says he is not listening to it. "I didn't notice the music, someone else had this car before me. I don't like this kind of music, but you know . . ."

OutKast sings about Rosa Parks, and Franklin, oblivious, comments over the lyrics about New York, the local Comfort Inn, and the weather.

When we arrive at the Comfort Inn, Franklin says, "This Comfort Inn is the poor Comfort Inn. This part of the highway is where black people generally stop, close to the bus station."

Coulda fooled me. Highways, most highways appear indiscriminate.

The next day, another day of sightseeing and research. A perfect blue sky, huge. We begin by visiting the Confederate White House, one of Jefferson Davis's many presidential suites throughout the South. The South's White House kept changing places as the South further redefined itself.

Huh?

There are bouquets of cotton stalks, beautifully placed throughout the many rooms of the small mansion. White visitors walk in and out and Chelsea and I must look odd there. Looking, no, studying the moth-worn and rusted Confederate paraphernalia. Two worlds that get along better than they pretend to: us, them, then, now. How intoxicating it is to pretend. How confusing it is not to.

A few blocks away from the White House is the Dexter Avenue King Memorial Baptist Church. No one is here but us, no tour guide. A peaceful place, compact. I take photographs of the sanctuary's crimson drum-traps set.

From there we move across the street to the Civil Rights Memorial in front of Southern Poverty Law Center. Maya Lin and black stone, but this time water and an etched list of some of the many ineloquent black people who died along with a few of the heroic whites that had easier lives to live and lose. We head back to the Rosa Parks Museum.

Today the museum is open. A young woman named Danielle conducts a tour, literally screaming to the crowd of Chelsea and me and a woman and her two daughters. At the end of the very loud tour I walk up to Danielle and ask her what she really thinks may have happened forty-six years ago on that bus. She confesses, without raising her voice, to hearing rumors about Claudette Colvin, "pregnant or not, ugly and ineloquent, but so what." Rosa Parks was actually only one of many who had refused to give up a seat during those deeply segregated times. Everyone knows that by now.

Yeah, I say. I've heard that Claudette woman is still pissed.

In the many photographs of Rosa Parks in the museum she looks like an upstanding school teacher. Danielle has suspicions and whispers, "Maybe her bus ride with that particular bus driver was a set-up, being as how that was not that particular bus driver's regular route and shift."
I say, Really, you mean maybe it wasn't "a spontaneous moment of brave exhaustion?"

Danielle puts her finger to her lips, "Shhh . . . you gone get me in trouble."

Trouble? Naw, I think to myself, everyone knows that theory as well.

I ask before walking out if she knows where we can find Mose T.'s house. Mose Toliver, the folk artist, championed by Mrs. Nancy Reagan, whose work is not hanging on the walls of this museum.

Mose T. is not home. But his daughter and granddaughter are. They have voices like men; a deep throaty "Hello" and "Come on in" boom out from some dark inner sanctum. The daughter is sprawled out in the farthest-most back room like a big brown beached whale, watching television, or maybe the television was serenading her, like most people everywhere in America with not much to do. (I've heard it's also like that in parts of Japan.)

Mose T. has paintings covering every wall of every room in the house: watermelons, turtles, cats, and self-portraits, a few of his current subjects.

His great-grandson sits in the front room and watches me impolitely move from room to room scouring every crook and cranny looking for that ancient work that might be lost in the shadows. I tell him I'm not here to steal, just to discover. "Then it'll have to be next time," he mumbles. Mose T. was visiting his girlfriend, where he sleeps.

Kill the nigger-loving son of a bitch!

On the way back to our motel our first white taxi driver of the whole trip yells from the driver's seat back to us, excited, "I want y'all to see somethin'. I'm gonna show you somethin' you won't believe, an ol' boy with a shopping cart full of garbage."
He makes a quick right turn and slows the car down.

"Look at him, got enough garbage to drown himself. We call him Mr. Comfort. I love the sight."

A guy with a shopping cart full of garbage is a major local tourist sight. A young black man on a street corner with a shopping cart filled with voluminous plastic bags. The man has dreadlocks.

"Hey!" the driver shouts at the man, and then laughs.

The man with dreadlocks waves back, smiling.

Do you have a large homeless problem here? I ask.

"Nah, we got folks that's lazy, just don't wanna work."

The whole time I imagined he was biting his tongue to keep from saying, "Look at that damn crazy nigger." I heard it anyway, the way he laughed and spit, and in his aggressive delight in showing us Mr. Comfort.

I bite my tongue and ask if he knows where the old bus station is. I wanted to elaborate but didn't. The one where John Lewis and James Zwerg and others were beaten to unconsciousness. Was he there? One of the hundreds of men, women, and children that suddenly appeared out of nowhere? That's what I wanted to ask but didn't.

I ask if he could take us there.

He replies that it's not operating anymore.

Yes, I know.

"The best thing about it is the neon dog on top—still works. At night it runs," he says.

He takes us there. "Look at it run!" It could have been art to him, like Mr. Comfort could have been art to him, a different art. Maybe he didn't, wouldn't, and couldn't have known that. I wondered what he'd think of the installations we created in all of our motel rooms, for the very certain anonymous audience of housekeepers.

The young Indian receptionist at the Comfort Inn has been in the American South all her life. "I love the South. I was in Atlanta first; I like Alabama better, less people." She drives a BMW. Her family also owns the nearby gas station.

And then there's Neal. Neal is also from India, blue-eyed, contact lenses, which irritate his eyes. He's a housekeeper and not from the same family and caste as the young receptionist. I make a motel room installation specifically for him, for Neal, the one housekeeper along the way with whom I felt I had a conversation. I suppose this was cheating, but hey:

Installation #10
A table set up with white bread, hot sauce, salt, pepper, plastic cups of water, paper plates, plastic knives and forks. And a paper bag with pocket change inside. (When I was young my mother would give me money and send me to the grocery with a list of items to buy. The grocer would put whatever change was left after shopping inside the grocery bag along with whatever I had bought from my mother's list.) The table set-up was missing a very important element, and that was the question of the installation. I left a list of possible missing items. Please check one:
    1. Fried Chicken
    2. Catfish
    3. Bar B Q Ribs
    4. Vegetable Curry
    5. Other
Plus a blank postcard and an offer of fifty dollars to coax Neal's reply.

Chelsea and I check out. And meet Neal in the lobby, before he walks into our room, to clean it, to discover his installation. He asks me to come back to Montgomery soon so that he and I can go to Florida together. Which part of Florida he doesn't say.

We are late to the station and miss our bus to Selma. It's not helping that the attendant cannot read her bus schedule and then will not yield to her confusion. She says that once we board a bus out of Montgomery we'll have to travel from Montgomery to Selma back through Montgomery to Birmingham before going down and across to Jackson. On the station time board it clearly lists a bus from Selma to Meridian to Jackson. She says the time board listing does not apply to us, today, gives some complicated, incoherent reason in very few words. Another attendant nearby, eavesdropping on the growing intensity of our conversation, walks up to the desk and says that there is a bus from Selma to Jackson, leaving Montgomery in four hours. The woman then empathically agrees, "Yes, that's what I said all along!"

We have four hours to wait and so hop into a taxi and pay another visit to Mose T., hoping he'll be home this time. He is, sitting on his porch, animated, eighty-something with a mouth full of real teeth. He paints everyday. Neighbors come up almost hourly, walk into his house (like I did days before) and shop for angels, crosses, and watermelons. Today, mostly angels, which he has pretty much sold out. "Try back next week, maybe then I'll feel like paintin' some angels, maybe."

Mose T. does not really like talking about painting.

"I had 1,000 pounds fall on me, a slab of marble. A few years after that I fell from a ladder, four or five stories. Then my wife hit me with a stick. I'm all broke up. Not getting around as well as I should." Mostly he wanted to talk about his house, how he's rebuilt it, how the city will most likely tear it down for a new highway, how he bought and fixed up another house directly behind this one, how he told the city he's ready to move right now, he's just waiting on a check.

I ask anyway. Why do you paint and may I call you Mose?

"'Cause I can't do nothin' else. Used to plant flowers and trees but my body can't do that work no more. Was really good at it. Anyway, so now I just paint. Did enjoy going to the White House, Mrs. Reagan invited me. Had a fine meal, ate whatever I wanted, a fine meal." The four hours go by quickly.

At least we had good music when the Negroes were demonstrating.

Selma was another city not on the Freedom Bus Rides map. The organizers thought about it but concluded it would be too dangerous to go there. Later there was "Bloody Sunday" on Selma's Edmund Pettus Bridge.

Selma. Shockingly cute, darling, quaint, and the bridge looks like a toy.

Found a Goodwill store where I bought a pair of ancient overalls permanently pressed, and some record albums, like *Madman Across the Water* by Elton John, *Day-O* by Harry Belafonte and the Royal Scottish Bagpipes' *Amazing Grace*, and a few others, and walked across the Edmund Pettus Bridge, dropping them at strategic points along the way. All I could think to do there. An art prayer.

There are lots of ways to pray.

A Big Black Woman in Her Forties: "Don't pray for someone when you're out doggin' yourself."

Bus Driver: "Yeah, always stirrin' up junk."

A Big Black Woman in Her Forties: "He should stay home with his wife."

Bus Driver: "I don't think she wants him there."

A Big Black Woman in Her Forties: "I wouldn't neither."

Bus Driver: "The women who marry those men in politics would never leave them but don't care if those men are home or not. Got them big ol' houses all to themselves!"

A Big Black Woman in Her Forties: "Ya got that right."

Bus Driver: "I tells it like it is."

They were speaking of Jesse Jackson and President Clinton, I suppose; don't know what started it. The white lady bus driver drove a UPS truck for many years before becoming a Greyhound bus driver.

"This is only my second job, drivin' all these people to Mississippi!"

But Medgar ain't home.

Tony, from Veterans Cab Company, a young black man, thirty-five, isn't sure where Medgar Evers's house is located. He knows the neighborhood, same Jackson neighborhood where he grew up, he just doesn't know where the house is. He calls in to his dispatcher,

"Where's Medgar Evers's house?"

"Don't waste your time son, Medgar ain't home," the dispatcher chuckles.

Tony also finds the joke kinda funny, laughs, and says, "Fuck him, I got a friend who lives in the neighborhood. He'll give us directions."
To a soft green ranch-style house, unmarked, kept up as though Medgar were home. A nice neighborhood. A suburb when Medgar lived and died. With a small open field across the street, a few houses down, where I imagine Byron De La Beckwith barely hid in the grass, and shot, inhaling the sweet air of night honeysuckle.

I bow in the driveway of 2332 Margaret Walker Alexander Drive where Medgar Evers was assassinated.

On the way back downtown Tony shares some of his heritage, "There was a Klan march in '91 down Amite. We turned them back. I'm proud of that day. I tell my son that I was there, I was there. No one's gonna take that away from me. But you wanna know something?" shaking his head mournfully. "There was a brother marching with the Klan."

A black man? I say, incredulous.

"A brother! Couple brothers. I kid you not. And they weren't driving no bus neither. A sad day. Black folks who hate black folks. 'Then come on boys, march with us.' They don't know that when the Klan runs they gone leave their asses behind."

Tony recalls another incident, as perverse, about another pair of black men, not the same ones marching with the Klan, but two other black men marching in front of the court house wrapped in rebel flags, supporting the State's opinion on keeping the flag as a State symbol. Still digesting the Klan account I have absolutely no response to this second tale. Both of these stories quickly become part of my new Southern mythology. The truth or fiction of it doesn't matter.

"I like to talk to the old people," he says. "They couldn't wear shorts in the summer downtown. They had to put paper towels around their heads when they tried on hats downtown. They were hosed walking back from church on Sundays. The police would throw black boys off this bridge, here, if they were uppity troublemakers. In Kokomo, a small town down south, they just lynched a sixteen-year-old boy who they said raped a little white girl, happened six months ago. Sometimes I drive my taxi to these small towns and it's like nothing has happened in the last forty years. Black folks cookin' for white people when they could be cookin' for their own businesses. Grinnin' and everything. I was in Kokomo recently, near where the boy was lynched, 'cause he was dating two white girls out in the open. Rebel flags flyin' from every house, white folks lookin' at me funny. It got dark and I drove 125 miles an hour outta there. Shit yeah, I was scared. Got a $300 ticket gettin' outta there, sure did. Yep, things are still bad here, but you know what? I ain't pickin' no cotton, not like my parents did."

BLACK SOUTHERNER IN GRAY

I ask him, naively, where are all the cotton fields today?

"I don't know. I think most of them were turned into catfish ponds."

He drops us off at a restaurant near Farrish Street, says he has heard that it's good but that he has never been there himself.

Mayflower Café. The whole kitchen staff is black. In the dining room, one black bus boy and three thirty-something blonde waitresses, all very cordial. There's a white matronly cashier. The owner is a small round white man who spends some time in the kitchen and some in the dining room. Outside the restaurant stands a fully dressed cop: black riding boots, aviator sunglasses, the classic cap. A doorman. I have flounder stuffed with crab meat. Chelsea has the spaghetti.

The Mayflower is not far from Farrish Street, the famous and run-down once-upon-a-time black Mecca of Jackson, like Second Street in Richmond. There are only white customers joining us in the Mayflower. But plenty of black strollers walking by the windows—thus, the fancy doorman I suppose. As we leave the restaurant the police officer says, and I kid you not, "Ya'll come on back now, ya hear," winking under his sunglasses.

The young black receptionist back at our motel had also recommended the Mayflower. Said she'd never been there but heard it was good.

I had also asked her, naively, where were all the cotton fields today?

"I don't know. I think most of them were turned into catfish ponds. Maybe there's more money in raising catfish than in growing cotton," she said.

(Years later many of the catfish farmers across the South would be draining their artificial catfish ponds due to the high cost of feed. Waiting for the next iteration, maybe soybeans, or corn, or "tumbleweed.")

"No mob greeted us at the Jackson bus terminal," recalled Frederick Leonard. "As we walked through, the police just said, 'Keep moving' and let us go through the white side. We never got stopped. They just said 'Keep moving,' and they passed us right on through the white terminal into the paddy wagon and into jail."

The Freedom Riders never made it to New Orleans. Too bad. New Orleans would have been an interesting place to land, after all the trouble, New Orleans being more abstract than the rest of the South and, like New York City, not like any other place in the U.S. Staid and amorphous, a self-contained and culturally unreliable environment affected by centuries of unpredictable human activity.

So it should have been no surprise that there are very few places in New Orleans where one can shop for musical instruments. I want to buy a trumpet. (Because I couldn't get a hold of the trumpet W.I. used to play and New Orleans is where the trumpet became infamous, a weapon and protection.)

There used to be pawnshops everywhere where you could trade and sell old beat-up coronets, guitars, saxophones. The pawnshops are still there but now they deal primarily in jewelry.

After a half day of searching we are directed to two stores that merchandise musical instruments. One has no used trumpets and the other has a few. I buy a perfectly beat-up Bach trumpet at the one that has a few. Someone has played the shit out of it, but it sounds good to me and it looks even better, the way it's all banged up.

During the thirties and forties my grandfather, W.I., played trumpet in his traveling troubadour band in South Carolina. Popular tunes of the time. On the weekends he'd get drunk and blow the blues. He would pawn the trumpet every few months. Had pawned it right before he died.

Mama Bill, my grandmother, got it out of the pawn shop after my grandfather died, held on to it until she died and now my Uncle Trent says he has it in his attic. My grandaunt Mattie says Trent doesn't have it in his attic, that he sold it long ago, although she can't prove it.

Let's go home, I say to Chelsea. And I think about all the other things that happened that I didn't really write about: the rituals; the installations in our motel rooms; the micro performed/peripheral movement studies in the bus-station waiting areas; the cartoons which I then copied onto postcards, cryptically, and postaged, unsigned, assassin-like, to the officials giving me money for this adventure. Scaring them, I hope. The only overt audience to any of this.

Chelsea videotaped everything, the proof. And every morning she'd ask me a single question, her own private research, standing behind her video camera, about race or backyards, what I remembered growing up. My answers were very tentative, deflective . . . but I did tell her this story one sleepless night in Jackson. I woke her up . . .

Dave's Superette Story
. . . When I was a kid I would run. In the beginning it was simply how I got from point A to point B. It began with a race with my father when I was six or seven on a long track of grass on the side of my grandfather's house on Cleveland Avenue. My father was young and seemed to me idolatrously fast. He won the race deliberately and left me crying fifty yards behind. This measurement became the world's longitude. I now had something with which to measure my dull innocence. I became my mother's messenger. I would collect her small change in my palm and run until I had arrived to the same places, mostly Dave's Superette, paid for, collected, and returned with whatever provisions she requested.

Inside my house I would run up and down the stairs to and from the second floor or to and from the basement, but I would never run inside the remainder of the house, the flat surfaces. Running remained my private practice. One evening after school, wearing long pants and hard brown shoes, I ran around the track for hours until there were no other boy runners in sight and no more sun. It was a breakthrough.

I've run from cars pelted with eggs, drunken jocks wanting to fight anything not running, not moving. I've run from police searching for young black shoplifters, and I've run from grave-yard ghosts, real ones. Somewhere near the beginning, I ran a mile, screaming for my mother, with a dart protruding from my stomach, a projectile tossed by a boy I barely knew trying to get my attention at a different neighborhood playground. Twice I ran out into traffic, chasing pre-adolescent spirits. And twice I'm certain I almost died.

1. A chrome bumper screeching and stopping close enough for me to stare down it's green Indian chief hood ornament and pushing me sideways, tripping, breaking my bantam-legged rhythm.

2. My pet dog grabbing the seat of my pants and pulling me back enough to the curb so that I could feel the breeze of a speeding metal blur on my face.

"Well, when the Indians attacked, we always put the wagon in a circle and fought from between the wheels. I thought that if every wagon carried a long plate with rifle holes, the men could stand the plates on the outside of the wheels when the wagons were in the circle and be protected. It would save lives and that would make up for the extra weight of the iron. But of course the party wouldn't do it. No party had done it before and they couldn't see why they should go to the expense. They lived to regret it, too."

Jody looked at his mother, and knew from her expression that she was not listening at all. Carl picked at a callus on his thumb and Billy Buck watched a spider crawling up the wall.

John Steinbeck, *Red Pony*

Race and Backyards

August 1, 2001

I've walked past the obscure architecture bookstore on lower Lafayette Street many times before, but this time I stop and gaze through the window to see a young Asian woman wearing cut-off denim shorts cornrolling the Afro of a young black man sitting behind a computer at the front desk.

I walk in, pretending to stoop lower than the low doorway actually is, and ask if I could be next, even though I'm not wearing an Afro, not nearly. She laughs, he doesn't. I don't really browse.

"Better watch your head on the way out," he says.
Thanks, I'll be sure to do that, I say, turning around, heading for the exit, gazing briefly at the books and magazines about buildings built to last centuries. (Or twenty to thirty years at most.)

September 10, 2001

Feeling little to no apprehension about any impending attack, I leave town without a premonition that something bad is about to happen. I don't even notice the weather, how gorgeous it is outside.

September 11, 2001

"Ohayo. It's early there. (Pause . . .) It's good that you are traveling, and not home. (Pause . . .) I am sorry. (Pause . . .) I will see you soon and that makes me happy." That's all she really says . . . it is perfect.

September 20, 2001

Asako was born in Niigata, Japan. I've never seen her in cut-off denim shorts and she does not know how to cornroll hair.

Asako, what do you think about when you think about home, the concept of home?

"The place you share food with somebody. First thing came to my mind was that. And it's important that the winters are not cold, like they are in Niigata," she answers.
So she and I share food where we are.

I still miss New York, I tell her.

Later, in a vast dry desert gloaming, I construct a series of tiny rock-mound memorials that no one will see and surely not recognize. I test my assumption and ask Asako to try and find them. She tries. "I think I found one," she tells me.

September 25, 2001

(On Being Prepared) You've got everything in here, I say, shopping for a flashlight at a hardware store on a Navajo reservation past Farmington, New Mexico, on the way to Four Corners.

"Yeah, we got everything," says a man with braids, standing next to the cashier, wearing a red cowboy shirt and jeans. "Even got AK-47s. I'll show you one for an orange soda," he whispers. A what?

"An AK-47 for an orange soda." The cashier then smiles.

OK, I'll buy you a soda if you show me an AK-47.

"Which one? We got a few," he says.

Any one of them, doesn't matter.

He and I walk to the back of the store. (Asako stays put near the front, somewhat confused why I would want to see an AK-47.) And right off a gun rack in full view, next to a row of light bulbs and pliers, he pulls out a not-so-handsome but very heavy rifle. "You wouldn't know it was an AK-47 unless you knew." It looks quickly manufactured, rough wood and steel.

"But so what," he says. "It gets the job done."

Wow, how many of these do you sell?

"Oh, we sell lots of these and lots of all the other guns you're lookin' at."

There are many. Strange shapes and sizes, all in the open, nothing locked or behind any kind of glass cabinet.

Do you have flashlights?

"Yeah, over there, next to the toilet paper."

Oh good, we need some of that too, I say.

The flashlight was on sale. Comes with a large new battery taped neatly on the outside of its yellow-shell body. I was looking for something smaller but this would do, plus it's on sale. I immediately take it out of its packaging and try to place the new battery inside the empty shell but can't get it to turn on. The cashier helps, and then the man with the braids helps, and five minutes later the flashlight works. I hand the cashier a twenty; she gives me change. I switch the light on and off a few more times before exiting the store. Say goodbye and thanks.

"What about my soda?"

Oh right, how much do I owe?

"Seventy-five cents."

Here's a buck.

"Much obliged," the man with braids says.

September 30, 2001

. . . The Southwest is something altogether different from the South all right, more confidence maybe. More flags, more guns maybe. Lots of flags at the moment and soap-lettered "We love America and New York" on SUVs and pickup trucks. And red, white, and blue collages, kid art, donning the walls of motel reception rooms. The word "America" has become like the word "nigger." It means this and then it means that, depending on the speaker, culture, and size of arsenal.

The Native Americans here fly the biggest flags, from what I can see. They also wear wide straw cowboy hats, Wrangler jeans, Dexter cowboy boots and drive Ford trucks the size of small houses.

The mountains and rivers and gorges of the Southwest are quieter, almost mute, do not care about what happened on September 11. Not a bit. The earth does not mourn, will not mourn. The ground remains hard and does not soften no matter how respectful one is, walking, sitting, setting up a tent, making love, sleeping. You wake up sore, tired, or peaceful and the ground is still hard.

An empty and dangerous countryside this is.

And then there are those who never even heard the news.

We meet a couple driving from Missouri to California. Very young, twenties, white. Driving a beat-up '80-something Ford station wagon. Destitute. Cans of Hormel Chili, old clothes, and gas vouchers from police stations litter the entire inside of their vehicle. Stuck in a gas station near Indian City, Arizona, hanging around asking for money 'cause their engine caught fire, 'cause the girl threw a tantrum the night before and jumped up and down on the hood of the station wagon, parked along a dark desert road, caving it in unto cables and fan belt and other stuff, igniting the engine. I give them ten dollars. They need fifteen more.

They tell us the whole story with more details than I want to hear. How he then gets really pissed, after she jumps on the hood and explodes the engine, and takes his wedding ring off and throws it into the dark night road. He was so happy he found it the next morning, glowing in the morning daylight. She says, "Yeah, damn, we almost lost our wedding ring."

He grabs her hand and then kisses her. "I had this dream last night," he tells her. "There were all these sheep on a cliff. One of them jumped. Then the whole herd followed. In the end, hundreds of dead animals lay on top of one another in a billowy white pile. 'There's nothing we can do. They're all wasted,' a nearby shepherd said. And then I woke up."

"Damn, honey, that's sick!" she says.

Later, Asako asks me to describe the dream again. At some point in the young man's telling she couldn't figure out what he was really talking about, a language problem, and she stopped listening.

"Are they in high school?" she asks.

I don't think so, I say. I think they're older than that. But younger too. (Misquoting a Dylan song).

Asako is fond of Bob Dylan. "When I was in high school," she said, "I would walk home from school, and on the way there was a record shop that for one whole year would play a blurry video recording of The Rolling Thunder Revue everyday, and everyday I would go inside and watch."

The young couple seems oddly sophisticated and really tough and kind of invisible, soft, these two, due to the enormous sky that surrounds them. In love with each other, the dust, air, sun, and all the hardness of this elevated unyielding ground.

He asks if I want to buy their Benson burner, one of their survival items, along with a flashlight and all the cans of chili covering the floor of the vehicle. I say no, 'cause then they'd starve and we already have our own flashlight. I'm also certain that they will sell the little stove later. Maybe they'll get five dollars for it, if they're lucky.

We use the flashlight we bought at the hardware store on the Navajo reservation for another week. Sometimes it doesn't work, won't light. Most times it does. We give it away. To a maintenance man at the rental-car return lot. Along with the leftover toilet paper, paper towels, fruit, and a small package of Handi Wipes. He tells me that our generosity has made his day.

Asako and I kiss each other goodbye. And she says the heat of the desert was nice but next time she would like more water, a sea, an ocean, or just more moisture in the air.

November 1, 2001
Flying has replaced running, I say to myself, sitting in the backseat of the taxi. The drive from the airport is dark and rainy. Can't figure out on which end of the island to look for smoke or no World Trade Center. The taxi driver points to the right direction and I see nothing but more rain and darkness. Disoriented and disappointed. "Those martyrs do it 'cause they think they will go to heaven, that's what they're told, where seventy virgins will service them. Well, in my experience, and I've been around, virgins are not fun. Seventy virgins would be a nightmare," the driver solemnly comments.

November 2, 2001
There are subterranean fires that they cannot put out. Put a music soundtrack to it, something foreboding or soothing, or something in between, and it becomes flamboyant fiction. That's what music would do.

BOB DYLAN

ARTHUR LEE

CHARLIE PARKER

DINAH WASHINGTON

ELLA FITZGERALD

TELL MAMA

ETTA JAMES

FRANK ZAPPA

JAMES BROWN

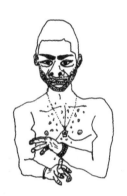

AL GREEN

JESSE MAE HEMPHILL

JIMI HENDRIX

LOUIS ARMSTRONG

SNARE DRUM

MAX ROACH

THE NOTORIOUS B.I.G.

MILES DAVIS

MISSISSIPPI JOHN HURT

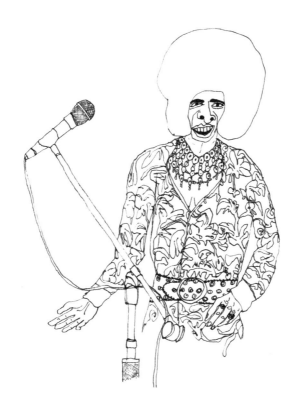

SLY STONE

ROLAND HAYES

MORRISSEY

SHIRLEY VERETTE

NINA SIMONE

Other Music Story (thirty-three years before the fires)

When I was sixteen two boys who seemed younger and who I had never seen before approached me at McCrae Park in Minneapolis, Minnesota, and asked if I wanted to join their rock band. I would be the lead singer. They were attracted to how skinny I was. Ninety-five pounds, I told them. At the moment there was no band; they were recruiting. They already had a name for the band, White Elephant. I was flattered, curious, but ultimately I knew it was impossible. My parents were Jehovah's Witnesses and I was under a very strict code of music. When we were at the Kingdom Hall, which is like a church without a steeple, we were allowed to sing from small pamphlets to piano music. I later heard from the composer Rhys Chatham, who also grew up a Jehovah's Witness, that much of the piano music played at the Kingdom Hall borrowed from Brahms. But the thought of being in a real rock band was exciting. My two other band experiences, if you could call them that, were lip-syncing the Beatles' "I Want to Hold Your Hand" in front of my sixth grade class with three other friends the Monday after their first appearance on *The Ed Sullivan Show*. A year later I tried to start my own band, whose only mimed song was "Money" by Bradford and Gordy. We had one rehearsal, as I recall. I was lead singer and played the tambourine. Both of these transgressions were done behind the sanctity of the Kingdom Hall's chorale. (A side note: two teenage girls from our Kingdom Hall ran away to New York to see the Beatles at Shea Stadium that first time in '65. It was a huge scandal, as though they had robbed a bank and disappeared, never to be heard of again.) I loved the rock and roll of the sixties. (I even liked the Fifth Dimension.) One year for a whole month, and it was winter, I think (it was always winter in Minneapolis, it seemed), I would sit at the kitchen table in the dark, huddled next to a radio, listening to Dylan's "Positively 4th Street," which seemed to come on the air every night at 8 p.m., while my parents watched television in another room. Later, in my bedroom, while everyone else was asleep, I would listen to Tony Glover's underground overnight radio show on KDWB, before falling asleep; more Dylan and Moby Grape, Love, Captain Beefheart, Zappa, Hendrix, Electric Flag, MC5, Quick Silver Messenger Service . . . long songs, unedited, indulgent, messy, the longer the better.

I told the boys no, that it would be impossible. They said, "OK, far out anyway." I don't remember ever hearing of any band called White Elephant. And I got better at pretending that I knew all the Kingdom Hall songs by heart.

I'm going away to a world unknown.
I'm going away to a world unknown.
I'm worried now, but I won't be worried long . . .

November 5, 2001
Dear L,

I had a thoroughly exciting phone conversation today with Nathaniel Kent, grandson of one of the Memphis pre-blues (or "post-antebellum black music") guys I've been listening and dancing to recently, Frank Stokes, "King of the Memphis Blues." His 1929 "How Long?" is my favorite three-minute pop tune to date.

Anyway, Stokes's daughter, Mrs. Helen Kent, still lives in Memphis, with her other son, Harold. Nathaniel was very friendly on the phone. I shared a little of my new project and he invited me to visit and talk, look at photos.

I thought it would be an opportunity to begin my "Dancing through the Delta" project, which will begin in Memphis, by offering the Kents a three-minute dance (in their backyard, garage, maybe kitchen?) to Frank Stokes's music. This no doubt will be interesting.

Love R

Dear R,

Here are my questions:

What did you do? Get your hands on a Memphis phone book and start making calls to all the Stokes in the book, one of whom happened to recall that Frank Stokes had a daughter named Helen, and that Helen Kent has a son named Harold?

So then you looked up Harold Kent and he's telling you to come over, and you're going to dance in the yard of Frank Stokes's daughter and grandson, and then you're going to sit on the porch and drink lemonade and look at old photos that no one in the world has ever seen. How does this happen? Did you go to Memphis last time around?

Love L

Overview

Memory mediates spatial transformations. In the mode of the right point in time (kairos) it produces a founding rupture or break. Its foreignness makes possible a transgression of the law of the place. Coming out of its bottomless and mobile secrets, a coup modifies the local order . . . Memory is a sense of the other. Hence it develops along with relationships—in traditional societies as in love—whereas it atrophies when proper places become autonomous. —Michel de Certeau, *The Practice of Everyday Life*

And no, I've never been to Memphis before. And no, I have no family in the Delta.

Routing a Reconciliation III (The Dancing and Dying Tour)
November 2001
Frank Stokes was a blacksmith, shoed horses mostly. Lived in "Shinytown" in Memphis. (Shinytown was really "Coloredtown.") He was tall, six feet two inches. Would tour to small towns, around Memphis mostly, play in backyards, house parties, for a few dollars.

"Always smiled when he played, that's what I remembered," says Mrs. Helen Kent, his daughter.

She tells me she has no photographs of Stokes, as an old man or a young man, or as a father or husband. All she has of his life is what she remembers.

"He told me to keep his guitar. I had it hid under my bed for a long time. Till it fell apart and then I threw it away. I regret that I threw it away, now. I regret that. It'd probably be in some museum if I hadn't tossed it out."

"Hardly anyone here now has heard a him," says Nathaniel. Nathaniel is in a reggae band named Exodus. "But there are lots of bands named Exodus," he says. "It's not been easy distinguishing ourselves. It's also been hard being in an American reggae band. We don't get the respect. They always say, 'What you doin' playin' reggae? You ain't from the island.'"

"What is it that you do, young man?" Mrs. Kent asks me, after telling us she's not heard Nathaniel's music, nothing of the reggae of his particular Exodus.
Well, I'm not so young and . . . well . . . here, I'll show you.

Chelsea and I ask for permission to retreat back to the car and retrieve our boom box, CD, and video camera. Back inside Mrs. Kent's house I dance for her, and Nathaniel and Harold, in their living room, to Frank Stokes's "How Long." It must seem strange. It certainly is for me. Mrs. Kent watching, doesn't tap her feet, her tiny body sunk (more like, swallowed) in her broad-backed upholstered chair. But I think it makes her happy, or at least amused. At one point she says, "He's dancin' to the whole thing," the whole three-minute song, a long time for her, maybe too long. I love this immediate response while I dance and then Nathaniel adds, "His dancing looks like it's tryin' to bust out to freedom." What he actually sees is my body desperately trying to stay within the narrow four-foot-wide path from the open front door and the eight or so feet to the kitchen entrance without bumping into any piece of furniture or sitting body. When I finish, Nathaniel asks if what I'm doing is "a Southern thing?" I tell him, panting, that I don't know what Southern is but what I hope I'm doing is bringing this music back to life. Mrs. Kent nods. "That was fun," she says.

Memphis is a city easy on the eyes. Has a sweet smell from the Mississippi River. And is small enough to keep us from getting too exasperatingly lost.

We have a huge rental car. A maroon Grand Marquis, a pimp car. Much too spacious for our purposes but perhaps appropriate for the streets of Memphis.

The historical enormity of the city has taken me by surprise. From Mrs. Helen Kent's house to the Lorraine Motel, now the National Civil Rights Museum, to Beale Street to Sun Records to Graceland, all in about twenty-four hours, has been slightly overwhelming.

"It ain't a bad place—must not be, 'cause I'm still here. Nope, ain't never heard of Frank Stokes or Furry Lewis neither. Nope, ain't never been to Graceland but I live right nearby. It ain't really a mansion, just a big house. I don't watch the house, but I like watchin' the people that goes to the house all year round, from everywhere," a trolley driver adds.

The emotionally kinetic journey from Mrs. Kent's house to Graceland is like going from a secluded forest lake to a netherworld basement with a swimming pool. From humble honesty to hyper-artificiality. Yep, and nope, it doesn't make any sense. Graceland is stuck in time, delusional, a daze. I bet it was that for Elvis as well. Gold records and more gold records, and shag carpet, and platinum records, and shag, and sparkling jumpsuits, and shag, with no window light anywhere that I can see. What a fucking life.

Mrs. Kent listens occasionally to a couple ragged re-issued albums of Frank Stokes's music that Nathaniel swiped from the public library, and two recently donated CDs from the Yazoo Records company in New Jersey. The family has no commercial rights to Frank Stokes's music (of course).

"I think there's more fear now from the black community here than there was forty years ago, 'cause now folks are afraid of losing what they have acquired since integration. Before they had nothing to lose. That's what I think," says Ida, a museum guide, in the lobby of the National Civil Rights Museum.

A middle-aged white man standing nearby nods in agreement and sadly announces, "Memphis has lost two kings!"

I counted three, I add.

Friday

A young woman curiously looks out from the door of a beauty parlor on Main Street, Como, Mississippi, a classic Southern railroad crossing town, two hours south of Memphis.

"Hi, my name's Ruby, Ruby Brown."

Hi, I'm Ralph; this is my daughter, Chelsea.

"So what are you doin' here? Not much to sightsee."

I ask if she's heard of or knows anyone who knew the musician Fred Mcdowell, Mississippi Fred Mcdowell, who used to live in Como. Ruby quietly thinks about the question for about thirty seconds . . . "Oh, Fred Mac!? I heard a' Fred Mac, many times . . . and I guess that was his real name, Mcdowell? Yeah, sure was. Well, you're in luck. I'm not working at the moment, lost my job, I can take you around to talk to the 'old timers,' who surely knew Mac, or were related to him. Ya'll are driving, right?" Absolutely, I say, a pimp car. "A what car?" she says, startled. Not really, only joking, you'll see, I say. Ruby, smiling again, turns and waves goodbye to the two or three friends in the parlor and we walk back to our car.

"Boy, it's so big in here," Ruby says from the back seat. Yes, palatial, I say. She directs us a few country blocks away from where we began.

There's an old concrete foundation that lies in front of a freshly painted white tract house that used to support the trailer home of Mississippi Fred Mcdowell.

Mrs. Mitchell lives next door. She has a framed dashing photograph of Mcdowell, which sits on a lamp table in her living room. He wears dark glasses and a wide-brimmed hat. Has a slight smile on his face. Mrs. Mitchell tells us that her cousin was married to Mcdowell. I say, Oh, is she singing on his first recording? She doesn't acknowledge the question, just smiles, a little confused. I ask if she'd like to hear the recording I'd just mentioned. I'll play it for you, I say, and excuse myself and go out to the car and bring in the boom box and the Mcdowell CD, his first one, recorded by Alan Lomax in the forties.

Mrs. Mitchell listens awhile to "Keep Your Lamps Trimmed and Burning" and concludes that the woman singing on the recording was his first wife, Annie Mae, not Mrs. Mitchell's cousin, his second wife.

I ask Mrs. Mitchell if I can dance for her, to "Going Down the River." I tell her I've been dancing to it recently in my New York apartment. A modern "buck" dance, I say. She says, "Yesss, please."

Can I videotape it, the dance? I ask. "Sure, why not, I guess my house is tidy enough." Chelsea retrieves the camera.

Staying within the truncated parameters of empty space created by the living room furniture, I dance. Mrs. Mitchell sits fixed, oddly entertained in her pink house robe, tapping her feet in her white cotton slippers. Ruby, sitting next to her, says, "Yeah, that's how they used to do it. I remember seeing that when I was a little girl, at one of Uncle Otha's parties." No, I think to myself while dancing, this is not how they used to do it, unfortunately, and I sure wish I could have seen what you saw back then.

Afterward Mrs. Mitchell reminisces, says the dances they used to do didn't have no names and that Fred drank a lot, but "what a sweet, sweet man he was—a share farmer, picked cotton early on."

I give Mrs. Mitchell the Mcdowell CD. She says she has only heard and danced to his music live. I don't have a case for the CD, left it at our motel, so she places it in her Como Yellow Pages. She has no CD player but says she has a grandson who might help her find a way to listen to it from time to time.

"One of his best friends, Uncle Otha, is still alive," Ruby says, as we get back in the car. "Not far."

Ruby's mother was raised by Otha Turner. The ninety-three-year-old master "fistes"(cane fife) musician—and a living link to rural blues and military fife-and-drum pre-blues that extended well into the nineteenth century. Ruby guides us to his barely put together house and farm in Gravel Springs. When we arrive, Otha is standing in his backyard, meditatively still, thinking about something. He looks at Ruby and barely recognizes her but then does. And then he begins to welcome us, a coded introduction part playful, part bored, part inspired. He plays his fife and sings a little, tells a few jokes, holds court for an hour or so.

Is this blues? I wonder, this improvised greeting. "There's too many expectations with playin' the guitar, audience wants to hear too much. With a fistes you only got two sounds. That's it." He puts the fistes in his back pocket and speaks briefly of his dear friend "Mac," Fred Mcdowell, how he slipped him a bottle of moonshine near the end when he shouldn't have. But mostly he talks about how expensive goats are today, now that "white folks get how good they are to barbeque." He says if he lives through next summer he'll have another big ol' weekend barbeque, Family Goat Barbeque Picnic, on Labor Day weekend. "With dancing and foot-stompin' music you ain't gone see or hear nowhere else."

We stand around kicking up dirt, Otha sings a little more, we talk, laugh, and hop about in his front yard till it gets dark. Say our goodbyes. Otha enjoyed the interruption I think. And for a moment it had stopped being about research.

We drive Ruby back to Como, back to the beauty parlor, say goodbye and head south to Clarksdale. Driving to Clarksdale on Highway 6 at eight o'clock at night is harrowing, utterly harrowing. I've never been on a road this dark before. And in my foreigner manner of thinking, Mississippi and dark don't go together.

In the lobby of the Hampton Inn the next morning there is a teenage boy preparing a cup of coffee with six packets of sugar and a couple packets of artificial sweetener, asking me questions in an English I don't understand. Finally, I make out, "Got a quarter?"

Hard to find work around here? I ask.

"You must not be from round here."

No, I'm not.

"You stayin' here?"

Yes.

"Can't wait till I'm twenty-one."

So how old are you?

He doesn't answer.

I walk back to my room to get five dollars. When I return to the lobby he's gone. I run out to the parking lot. Call out to him. We walk toward each other, he looks at me frowning, I hand him the five dollars, and he nods, turns and walks away, drinking the coffee, his breakfast, with one hand, putting the money in his pocket with the other.

Mae Smith, interpretation specialist at the Delta Blues Museum in Clarksdale, has a master's in communication from University of Mississippi. But she hosts the museum 'cause she wants to make sure that "they (mostly white men), those who started this museum, don't let their love of the blues get out of hand." She seems thrilled to see my daughter and me, says she's always so happy when black folks walk through the door. The museum has been opened for twenty-five years; she was hired six years ago, the first black staff person hired.

I buy new CDs of Fred McDowell, John Hurt, Otha Turner, Son House and ask why there are no CDs of Skip James and Jack Owen. She wonders aloud why I'm not interested in Bessie Smith. I tell her that Bessie Smith is too famous. And that we already drove past the gloomy rooming house here in Clarksdale, where she reportedly died unattended following a car accident, after a nearby white hospital refused to treat her.
I have a few Memphis Minnie songs I like a lot, I say.

She responds that there are other women blues artists I could listen to besides Bessie Smith and Memphis Minnie and then asks why we're going to Money. "Must know someone there," she concludes.

Looking for ghosts, I say.

THE noise of the fierce fighting
was heard far away in the deep
dark jungle. And at once they...
they all came smashing and crashing

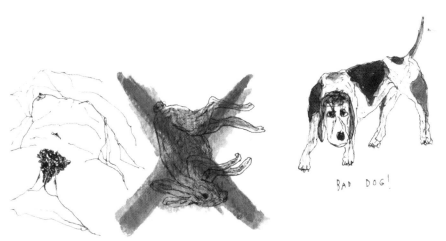

BAD DOG!

AT THE HUNT THERE WAS BELLOWING AND LOTS
OF SHOUTS OF SUCCESS, NOT SHOUTS OF JOY.

Sunday

It is hunting season, from Clarksdale to here, evident in the weather, countryside, and many pickup trucks with drivers wearing camouflage. Our map says it's nearby. Yes sir, Money, Mississippi. Know where it is? I ask a group of men, not wearing camouflage, sitting around a broken-down seventies Chrysler in a backyard, off a dirt road near Highway 8.

"You go back left and take the first left down the road with fresh blacktop. It'll take you all the way into Money."

Along the way we pull over in the dense shrubbery along the Tallahatchie River, calculating an imagined whereabouts, a borrowed remembering, an obscure naked floating body with "a gin fan attached to its neck." We take photos and video of a slow-moving muddy river that could be anywhere, against the brightly lit day and abrupt loud gunshots of unseen hunters. We nervously cut our documentation short. And drive down the blacktop eight more miles, slowly, funereal, Chelsea's suggestion.

In Money a shiny new dark blue pickup drives by, slows down, stops, and slowly backs up to where we're standing. A young white man wearing a complete and muddy hunting uniform, gets out of the truck. Smiling, he tells us to be careful with whatever it is we're doing, standing under the skeletal "Young's Grocery and Market" sign awning. "The building will come down soon, it's pretty rickety," he warns us, walks away, gets back into his truck, and waves goodbye. It is a shell, barely there and seemingly empty, like the town, hamlet, and indeterminate community. It is remarkably quiet here, right here, where for the moment not a single echo can be heard from all the many nearby deer rifles.

I improvise for the camera with "Bye baby," "Dar he," "I had no choice," phrases I remember from research. I place my hand in the dust in front of the dying doorway, the dead building, the mute hamlet; a witness. I also improvise with a Coke bottle and a whistle. Don't really know what else to do here, nothing else. Surely there's more I could have done.

Maybe I should have said, "He left me no choice." Emmett Till, that is, left Roy Bryant and J. W. Milam no choice, white savage honor, that is.

Later, I felt like I should have danced, but didn't. Didn't seem appropriate.

Money is silent, disappearing; Greenwood, Mississippi, is certainly not. That same day inside a brand-new blues museum in Greenwood, a country western radio station plays something twangy. Another earnest white blues enthusiast has recently put the place together. The museum has an impressive amount of Robert Johnson paraphernalia. It's more like a storefront gallery, homemade, where a young white woman, a cousin of the earnest white enthusiast, working behind the counter, knows nothing about the blues. "Yeah, I was really surprised to learn that some of the songs we sing at our church sound similar to the music I hear in here, very interesting," she says.

I ask her where Robert Johnson is buried, a very tricky question, I know. Nearby, I've heard. She doesn't know, of course. I ask her about Dockery, Mississippi, and then about Charley Patton. "Is that a city?" she asks. "I'm from Jackson and don't know much about these small towns," she apologizes.

Charley Patton, maybe the locus of the original trinity, I say. Patton, Son House, Robert Johnson. Patton, unlike the others, is more myth than real person. A lot of what's been said about him is probably not true. There is some truth. His music is radical, raw, and his lyrics incomprehensible. He reportedly was married eight times and reportedly had his throat slit when he was forty-two. He died of heart failure at forty-three. He wanted to be what we would now call a pop musician, a pop star. And he was, sort of. He reportedly played the guitar behind his back long before Jimi Hendrix did. He was popular in his time and traveled a lot but never made it to Europe, unlike Hendrix, B. B. King, and James Baldwin. Of course, none of this takes anything away from the importance of Robert Johnson. And Walter "Furry" Lewis and Mississippi John Hurt are also from the area, although Furry Lewis made his name in Memphis, I conclude. The young white woman behind the counter can only smile at all this new information.

Like clockwork, Chelsea is starving. It's lunchtime, and so we find a café down the street from the museum called BAR BQ, that doesn't have B-B-Q. The owner of the restaurant had a stroke and couldn't cook anymore so his wife took over and doesn't like preparing B-B-Q. We have fish sandwiches that are delicious. I think about dancing for her—it would be interesting here, around food, a kitchen, people eating—until she confesses to not liking the blues. She says she prefers fashion shows.

Next door to BAR BQ there's a shoe repair shop. Maybe I could dance here? An obvious outflow of the spontaneity from next door. I ponder it. (But unlike the quickly considered BAR BQ show that never happened, here I'm not thinking about an audience, not at all. And like the quickly considered BAR BQ show that never happened there's the issue of whose blues would go with this place, given that there are so many blues artists who come from this place, or nearby. But I suppose, if push came to shove, I could always run back to the local blues museum and buy some convenient Robert Johnson. All of this of course is hypothetical. At the moment none of these things are a consideration.)

We walk inside to a tiny waiting area in front of the shoe repair counter. There are two older black men talking, one sits in a chair, the other stands in front of a shelf of the usual shoe repair shop paraphernalia: shoe polish (in a few colors), leather conditioner, shoeshine brushes, strings, shoe horns, shoe trees, and a variety of insoles . . .

The one standing asks he if he can help us; his specialty is shoes, he says. I can see that, I say. I introduce Chelsea and myself and explain that, no, she's not my girlfriend; she's my daughter. The owner Mr. McKinney, a tall, well-dressed, and handsome man, has thirty-seven kids. He had his first child when he was thirteen, he says. The gentleman sitting is Mr. McKinney's best friend, who hasn't said a word yet and mostly looks down at my shoes. Neither seem particularly bothered by our (suspenseful?) entrance and its possible intrusion.

I begin to wonder which of us is the real audience. It's clear that this is not the time to break out into a dance. So I quickly change course. No, this is not about our shoes, I say. Actually, we're doing a survey, and I have a question about the blues, or what's left of the blues here in the Delta. Why is it that black folk aren't the ones opening these blues museums that seem to be popping up everywhere? I ask, exaggerating, improvising.

Mr. McKinney crosses his arms and looks down at his shoes, thinking about the question, while his friend continues to look at my shoes or Chelsea's shoes or something else on the floor.

"The blues were never really the blues anyway, so why bother with what never was," Mr. Mc-

Kinney says, abruptly, seeming somewhat disinterested in the question. And then the man sitting looks up and in a surprisingly sanguine voice says, "It has to come from the heart, when it does, it's pure. The music of today is for show."

Maybe that was not the right question, I think to myself.

The man sitting is Mr. King. He says he met Dr. King Jr. once. "We are only together in name, and that's where we split. He was for peace and I'm a fighting man, I'll hit back. But you know Dr. King sho' played a hell of a game of pool." Mr. King then begins to describe, in longwinded detail, what "a hell of a game of pool" is without describing how he knew Dr. King played a hell of a game of pool, never mentioning that he had seen him play or that they had ever played together.

Every once in a while Mr. McKinney makes a broad statement about life, interrupting Mr. King's pool pontifications and bringing the place to complete silence. Finding an opening during one of these silences, I ask Mr. King how he would define "pure." What's pure? I ask. "Thank God, for slavery!" And then, "Slavery made black people pure. That's why the old blues was truthful, for your information." He continues, "The Jackson Five used to be pure, in the beginning, but the green took over the family, and in case you didn't notice, they broke up." And, "Gladys Knight and the Pips, they were pure before they got rich and lost everything."

He says that the Native Americans were even more pure, "'The Indians fought and died while the Negroes laughed and multiplied.' You know, if we could just get ourselves together and vote, we'd be a force. Yes, we sure would."

There's a photograph of one of Mr. McKinney's thirty-seven children, hanging above the shop's cash register and counter—a daughter, college age. He shows us another photograph, one he has in his wallet, of his son, a teenager.

After this pause, Mr. King continued, "Ya know, Greenwood is named after Greenwood Leflore, a half-French half-Indian chief, who received the land on which Greenwood was built as part of the Treaty of Doak's Stand." Huh? Treaty of Doak's Stand? Who was Doak? I ask. "Well, if he was standin', he whatn't no black man, that's for sure." And then he laughs for the first time.

I stand and think this is a perfect time to dance, a perfect audience, and maybe Mr. King could let me know if I'm anywhere near pure . . . especially since I have no music, nothing, no blues anybody.

And then an elderly white lady walks in, dressed delicately, from another Greenwood era. She asks Mr. McKinney if her shoes are ready. "No m'am, they ain't, but sometime early next week for sure." "Well, I can barely wait, Mr. McKinney, you know how much I like your service."

Right outside of Greenwood, on the same road going back into Money, sits Little Zion Baptist, a little white church and graveyard that we passed on our way to and from Money into Greenwood. We didn't know then that Robert Johnson is purported to be buried there, not until Mr. King told us he had heard some rumors, the third place Johnson is purported to be buried in the delta region.

It's a pretty day. And I mark out a moderately complex stepping composition/score where I walk around and/or hop over marked and unmarked graves in search of Robert Johnson's third gravesite. "'Cause it's such a common name," Mr. King warned. We find no marked grave with the name Robert Johnson. We do find, in the back of the church, a sign with a name and number for "The Robert Johnson Memorial Fund." I copy the information into my notebook for later investigation. I also jot down this question: Why weren't more blues musicians lynched?

We drive on to Yazoo City, a couple hours from Greenwood, and pass a few more young camouflaged white men looking meaner, poorer than they did in Greenwood County and in Money, hanging out outside a convenience store with new trucks and bumper-sticker slogans, such as, "IF YOU DON'T LIKE MY REBEL FLAG YOU CAN KISS MY REBEL ASS!" We also pass an abandoned outdoor stage with bleachers, a very odd sight.

We stop at three motels owned by Indian émigrés, looking for the right price, and at one motel that was "AMERICAN OWNED, AND PROUD OF IT!" We choose a Days Inn run by Indians. We unpack our belongings and call the Robert Johnson Memorial Fund in Greenwood and speak to Sylvester Hoover, who offers to give us a Robert Johnson Tour: to his gravesite at Little Zion and the site where he "spent his last minutes on his hands and knees, barking like a dog, and then died," and then to a nearby hotel, "where he once stayed when he was healthy." "Anytime," Sylvester says, even on Thanksgiving, but he'd prefer to do it any day but Thanksgiving. We decide it's best to meet day after tomorrow.

That evening, Chelsea's not feeling well, is off her insistent eating clock. She falls asleep early, to the televised sounds of *Buffy the Vampire Slayer*. After a few hours she wakes up, feeling a little better, "starving" in fact, and begs for a burrito.

I run across dark Highway 49N to the Taco Bell.

"Where you from?"

New York.

"I bet this town's a little small for ya?"

No, not at all.

"I bet it's too dark for ya?"

Huh?

"When I moved here from Chicago it was too damn dark! Now I kinda like it."

She hands over the 7-Layer Burrito, and I smile and walk out the door into the definitely too damn dark.

The next morning I enter our room with two cups of tea and overhear Chelsea, who seems to be feeling completely better, speaking to housekeeping:

"Do you like working here?"

Ruthee answers, "Don't like my boss. Always complaining. Always lookin' to see that I'm working. And I always have to tell him why I sometimes have to refuse an order that he gives. And if we're at the same place at the same time and he sees a piece of litter on the site, he'll say, 'Ruthee, pick that up.' What, he can't pick it up himself? But he's learnin', learnin' how to deal with us. Some of us here have told him a thing or two, about America, that yeah, we're black all right, but this ain't India."

Hello, Clementine? Hi, it's Ralph Lemon. I'm the one that called about that lynching? The one that occurred here in the twenties, a man named Willie Minnifield. "Oh, yesss, I remember you. Come by anytime. I'm here most days."

Clementine Davis directs the Oakes African American Cultural Center in Yazoo City, a kind of freestyle antebellum mansion, originally built by a freedman and his wife, modified many times from the 1850s to now and not on the historic District Yazoo City Walking Tour.

She tells me she's not heard of the "mass exodus of ten thousand colored persons from the vicinity of Yazoo City on August 11, 1923, following the burning at the stake of Willie Minnifield in a swamp near Yazoo City."

But she says she knows of one or two other lynchings that occurred while she was growing up in Yazoo. "A relative of mine was lynched, I think, " she says.

But if 10,000 black people fled this town-area in 1923, surely that event would have been remembered and passed down, I prod.

"Nobody I know ever talked about it, and I been here all my life."

Clementine was a schoolteacher for forty years. And wonders why the education system in Yazoo City, which is primarily black, does not access the African American Cultural Center hardly ever; maybe once or twice they've come by for a tour.

I ask her if she likes the blues. She says she likes all kinds of music, country western, Charlie Pride, Macy Gray. She asks what I do, who I am. I offer to dance for her. She happens to have a boom box with a Skip James CD in it. Skip James? I say, a little incredulous. "Yeah, he's almost a hometown boy, a celebrity." So I dance to that, to Skip James's "Drunken Spree," recorded in 1931. I have room after large room to choose from, and so the dance becomes that, a physical navigation through the first floor of an unlived-in and practically empty mansion, to the soundtrack of the molasses-like rhythm of Skip James, a music I have never danced to before.

Afterwards she claps. "I wish my niece had been here. Maybe y'all can come back and do this again." Well, I say, we saw this abandoned stage with a set of bleachers on Main Street, and I thought I would dance there on Thanksgiving Day, a memorial for Minnifield. You and your niece could maybe come by, be my audience? "Thanksgiving? I don't think that'll work. But any day other than Thanksgiving would be fine."

The Day after Tomorrow
We drive back toward Greenwood to meet Sylvester, for a tour of Robert Johnsonville.
We arrive at the church and graveyard a half hour early. We're ten minutes from Money, and I think maybe it's a good idea to drive back up the road to Money and explore another "opportunity" at the Emmett Till site. I wasn't satisfied with the earlier attempt a few days back. Surely there's more to say to the brutal murder that happened there. Chelsea is certain it will take too long to drive there and then back, but I assure her it's only ten minutes away, at most. We both know it will take at least twenty minutes. We drive back to Money, park in front of the barren storefront, and Chelsea documents my lips once again reciting "Bye baby," over and over, this time in an extreme close-up. That's all we do. I don't whistle, and no Coke bottle this time. We then speed back to meet Sylvester at Little Zion.

We make it back a few minutes late and wait. Sylvester never shows. And never shows. Two hours later, we drive back to nearby Greenwood to call him on a public phone at a gas station. He apologizes, says his son didn't show up for work, and he couldn't leave the Hoover Laundromat, his propriety.

OK . . . anyway, so where (the fuck) is it, sir, Johnson's grave?

"It's way in back of the church. Look for three pecan trees, two close together and one farther away. It's under the one farthest away. Look for some weather-worn plastic flowers, red and yellow, I think."

We drive back to Little Zion in early dusk. I begin to laugh as we trample through the Little Zion Baptist Church graveyard for the third time looking for an unmarked grave in a yard of dozens of them.

Chelsea, what's a pecan tree look like, like this one?

"I don't know, but I think they're a little more modest," she says.

Thanksgiving Day, Yazoo City, Mississippi

"Minnifield, who was found fishing in the swamp, was accused of attacking a woman with an axe at a point twenty-six miles distant. There was no indication to prove that he was the criminal. When the posse discovered him, he was in the company of another man. Both were seized and charged with the crime. Minnifield's companion escaped. Angered because he had slipped from their clutches, the mob prepared to burn Minnifield. He was dragged to a cleared space in the swamp, and a stake was driven into the ground until only his head was visible. A match was set to the brush, and as the flames crackled around the man, the woods resounded with the shouts of the mob."

Empty bleachers and a little stage inside the shell of an old building with no front facade or roof on Main Street. I dance on the stage, occasionally falling through the decaying plywood, to Mississippi John Hurt's 1928 recording, "Louis Collins." I don't know who Louis Collins is or was, and Mississippi John Hurt was from Teoc and Avalon, not Yazoo City, but the song seems appropriate, somebody mourning somebody else, its simple and hypnotic tone a sublime activation. Cars speeding by on Main Street, my audience. A three-minute blues dance, twice, a prayer maybe, to Mr. Minnifield, and to all those who had to run away, in truth or fiction. And then one more dance, but this time a freer movement experiment to the Pretenders' "Chain Gang," a hurling body dance just for me, bringing the episode a little more forward in time, while staying backward, I hope. The sky is a radiant blue. And not a single car nor person stops to watch.

Chelsea had been patient. It's 5 p.m. Thanksgiving Day and no eating establishment in the area seems to be open, not even Taco Bell. We drive around as far as we can before leaving the county and find a Sunshine supermarket just about to close. We quickly and desperately buy microwave turkey dinners, packaged vegetables, paper plates, plastic forks, knives and spoons, and Chelsea, thrilled, finds a pumpkin pie. (Yes, the Days Inn has a microwave.)

Not far from Yazoo City and two-and-a-half hours south of Robert Johnson's presumed third gravesite, ten minutes down the road from Money, is the quaint but oddly trendy hamlet of Bentonia, Mississippi, official population 390. A railroad crossing. Trendy 'cause it has one of the few remaining juke joints in the Delta, the Blue Front Cafe. It's famous on most of the virtual blues tour maps. Hometown of Nehemiah "Skip" James and Henry "Son" Stuckey, Jack Owens, and Buddy Spires, who still lives there and holds the Bentonia blues lineage. Along with Jimmy "Duck" Holmes, who has owned the Blue Front since 1976. A real, alive juke joint that has survived and continues to function.

In the mid-fifties the Blue Front was a mini-mart. The juke in the front, and in the back of the front room one could buy fruit, vegetables, shoes, and clothing. In the back room was a kitchen for hot dishes, and in a further back room was a barbershop. More recently, when Levi's filmed Jack Owens for a commercial in 1995, the director made sure all the Coke signs were removed, and the soiled ceiling and half-painted walls stayed in place, immaculately authentic, to a history that has not stayed in place.

Jimmy's house, a white, one-story ranch resting on a wide grassy lot, right off Highway 49, part of what had once been his father's sixty-acre farm, sits right next door to the original Blue Front owned by his father. Later it became the tiny-whitewashed shotgun house of Henry Stuckey.

Jimmy was five or six when he first remembers holding the giant guitar that belonged to Stuckey. Later, sitting in the front room of the house, taking lessons on his bright yellow plastic guitar, "I told him I wanted to sing like Elvis Presley, but Son Stuckey, he said, 'Naw, that's white folks. I want you to sing like me.' Stuckey taught me the Bentonia style, the same style he taught Skip James. You know, he had nine kids, something like that, and not a single person related to him knows a thing about his music. You talk to them and they don't remember nothing."

It is part of Jimmy's mission to explain over and over, as best he can, the difference between Stuckey and James and Owens. How Owens and James became famous and how there's not a single photograph of Stuckey anywhere, that anyone knows about.

The original Blue Front, what was once the home of Henry "Son" Stuckey, is now mute and exposed. Weather-washed of color. Inside, rooms with fallen clouds of yellowed insulation, and then an openness, free of critters because it's too cold, an openness holding on to skeletons of tables and faded upholstered chairs, a sink, a tattered reproduced painting of a bouquet of flowers still hanging on a leaning wall.

"Why are you here? Tell me again . . . ?" Jimmy asks, as he guides our tour.

Oh you know, research, I say, I might write a book. If I had known him better I might have said this . . .

I've come south, again, this time to research what might be left of the environment of the Delta blues and to dance in the living rooms, yards, and available spaces of those surviving friends, children, and grandchildren, along a slice of Mississippi's back roads, encountering some of the haunted ones (and what to do there?). A personal project, a counter-memorial, a meditation.

Every morning I stretch and warm up in the narrow space between the double beds of a Days Inn or a Comfort Inn, or a Motel 8 or 6, sometimes a Hampton Inn, from Memphis all the way to New Orleans, in preparation for an opportunity to dance for someone, even the ghosts. Sometimes it happens, sometimes it doesn't. But there is magic in this spontaneity. There is also preparation for this spontaneity, making myself available for a conversation, where both parties are saying yes.

For instance:
Here, I want to show you something that comes from the big city.
And here, I want you to hear something from down here that you already know about that I discovered back in the big city.
Or here, I want to give you something that is about both places and possibly beyond, up there and down here.
And then you say, "Although, I'm not quite sure what it is you're doing here, yes, I accept. And you can even photograph this moment. Sure, why not?"

"Welcome is every organ and attribute of me," sings the *Leaves of Grass*, Whitman.

"Who?" he says.

Walt Whitman, I say.

And then I say, Yes, why not? I can assure you, I know a lot about creative formality, conversing with society, and can afford to bring some artificiality to these grassroots convergences, making the scared mundane more vivid. Now, if that sounds interesting, let's get on with it.

So, Buddy Spires, of Bentonia, Mississippi, the blues harp partner of Jack Owens, tells Jimmy "Duck" Holmes, over the phone, that if his visitors want to hear him blow the harmonica it will cost us twenty dollars. Five dollars extra to video.

Jimmy points out Buddy Spires's yellow shotgun house from the Blue Front, across the railroad tracks, tells us we have to pick him up and bring him back to the Blue Front.

Buddy Spires is sitting in the draped late-afternoon darkness of his front room, wearing huge black sunglasses, putting on pomade and greasing his hair back with a comb. Once finished, he neatly places the comb on a side table, next to the jar of pomade and puts on a white Royal Crown baseball cap, with a purple brim.

How long you been playing the harp, Buddy?

"Since I was five, a gift from Santa. I got a harp and a BB gun, that's all I wanted. Harps didn't cost but a quarter. You could buy 'em at the drugstore. BB guns was five or six dollars. Things are expensive now. But I ain't bought a harp in a long while; tourist folk come round and give me harps for free. Guess I don't know if there's anything to miss about them ol' days."

Do you miss Jack Owens?

"God yes. We had such good times, so many experiences together. Been two years. I try to keep my mind in the present, but then I'll start to think about him . . . Didn't think what we was doin' all those years was anything, but people come around and wanted to hear us play. We been to California, twice, New York, once, Chicago, once, and where is it where it's really cold? Not Iowa, been there, once. Iowa weather is cool, not too cold."

Minnesota? Wisconsin? Canada?

"Nope, been to those places, all once. I can't remember where, but Jack and I arrived in short-sleeved shirts, and it was so cold the producer had to buy us some coats."

Buddy still finds this incident funny and laughs, his whole body shaking.

I ask if there is anything special about Bentonia harp music and he says no. Said he trained himself and just happened to be living in Bentonia; in that way his music had a Bentonia style. And then he mentions, as though it weren't very important, his awesome father, Arthur "Big Boy" Spires, who lived and played the blues in Chicago, excluding him from a Bentonia style altogether and making him famous, more famous than Henry "Son" Stuckey, Jack Owens, and Buddy.

We drive Buddy back to the Blue Front. I buy him a beer, and he sits and waits, telling jokes about preachers, the devil, and rabbits, while Jimmy plugs in his electric guitar and a couple microphones. (Jimmy prefers the acoustic guitar, his "baby," but it is missing a string. Jimmy, who was a student of Jack Owens, says Owens only played acoustic. Owens did at times play an amplified guitar. But I knew what Jimmy meant.)

"After Son Stuckey, Jack was my guru," Jimmy announces. "Whenever anyone asked Jack where his blues came from, he'd say from working in the cotton fields or behind a mule. 'What else you'd expect a man would think about, workin' like that?' he'd say. You know, the most amazing thing about the old blues musicians? Something no one ever talks about? They were all illiterate. Couldn't read or write a lick! Would make their songs up in their heads, in cotton fields, behind mules, sometimes before going to bed. And the next morning they'd have the song, ready to play."

Bentonia blues, open E, high wailing. "Nobody knows how the tuning got this way, but this is what makes Bentonia style so compelling," Jimmy continues, almost ready to play. (Actually, I'd read that Stuckey discovered the open E-minor tuning while a soldier in France during World War I, from soldiers he took to be Bahamians.)

A baleful sound. Startling, in how it refuses to entertain. And then that high-pitched singing. James had it, Owens had it, and Jimmy replicates it: "Son Stuckey, too, had a real tenor voice, you had to, no amplifiers in those days."

Buddy just blows the harp, a precise and muddy rage, without style, in complete love, in between beers.

Jimmy and Buddy play and I try to dance for a song, a slow heavy song, much slower and heavier than Skip James's "Drunken Spree" at the Oakes mansion, Clementine's place, but a song just as vital. A rhythm that now seems to drag on the floor. A hard floor. I dance and Jimmy and Buddy play, oblivious, and the onlookers watch and nod, oblivious. I disappear. I am invisible and the only one surprised.

As it gets dark, Mama B walks in. She's eighty-two. A town legend. A thin, boney beautiful woman, with short-cropped gray hair wearing a shimmering floral summer dress. "Been drinking straight whiskey and smoking everyday of her adult life and can out-dance anyone in town. An inspiration," Jimmy says. "A juke-joint lady and still alive to talk about it, or not, depending on her mood." Mood and character . . . and circumstance. I wonder what choices were made or not that brought her to this exclusive dark men's world, this history? Courage or something else, something more brittle?

She and Buddy sing, and later Mama B dances and more male bodies show up, and suddenly the whole place is awake, loud and noisy and smoky and drunk . . .

And still too damn dark outside as we drive back to the motel, our last night, heading for Jackson in the morning and then on to Meridian.

Jackson, Mississippi, is forty-five minutes south of Bentonia.

In the parking lot of the Hampton Inn off Highway 55 next to the fairgrounds, six or seven young Southern cowboys and girls are having a party, pull a gray legless dummy steer out of the bed of a white Ford pickup, leaving the tailgate open, and take turns roping the dummy cow from a distance of maybe fifteen feet. The truck radio is thumping OutKast or maybe Bubba Sparks. The new South.

The Jackson Fairgrounds became the "Fairgrounds Hotel" during the civil rights movement of the sixties, becoming a substitute for the over-crowded jails. Marchers of all ages were detained in the livestock exhibition spaces and pens.

There are no plaques or monuments commemorating that moment at the Fairgrounds today, but one can still see the pampered and overfed hogs.

November 26, 2001
Ninety-one miles straight east of Jackson sits Meridian. The Jimmie Rodgers Museum is in Meridian, less than a mile from our motel. "The Father of Country Music." "The Blue Yodeler." I buy a CD and a T-shirt, assuming these items may come in handy—a soundtrack and costume, a disguise perhaps.

From Meridian we drive up 19 toward Philadelphia, admiring the two lanes, the pristine scenery.

The Neshoba County Fairgrounds peak the circle from Philadelphia, down Highway 19, right on Route 492, to Route 21, back toward Philadelphia.

In Philadelphia we stop at a drugstore for directions to the site of the old Neshoba county jail. The druggist asks us which old jailhouse we're looking for, there are a couple, he says, suspiciously. The main county jail of the 1960s, I say, remaining vague because it feels appropriate, where the three civil rights workers were held. "Not sure what you're actually referring to, sir, but there was an old jail on Myrtle Street, just around the corner. Walk out the door and take a right," he tells us, a little vague as well. We walk around the corner, and a car stops us and a black woman, head out the car's window, asks us if we've found the old jailhouse. News obviously gets around and we tell her no, and she points to a one-story building directly across the street from where we're standing. There are three or four people in front having a discussion about something that had obviously just transpired inside, some business transaction, formal, courteous.

We stand peering. A woman from the group looks our way and asks us what we're looking for. Staring directly at the address of the building, I ask if this is 422 Myrtle, and she says, "Yes, it is." I thank her and walk away, embarrassed, frustrated that people are blocking my camera view, that I am there gawking at such a charged site in front of a small group of white people. I walk away to the corner of the block, leaving Chelsea holding her video camera, very confused. The small group in front of 422 Myrtle begins to disperse, and the woman who had earlier asked what I was looking for walks inside the building. Chelsea stands her ground the whole time, wondering what to do with the video camera. After a minute or so I walk back toward the front of the building just as the woman who had asked what I was looking for comes back out of the building and asks again what we're looking for. Now that she's alone I find the emotional space, courage, to explain my predicament.

She says, "Yes, this is the old jailhouse," and then asks would we like to look inside before she locks the building and leaves for lunch.

A low-ceilinged building. "It's been remodeled, ten years ago. This company's been here for three. The cells were in the back, I think. You can see where the iron doors stood. Yeah, this is where the civil rights workers were, I've been told," she said with some dispassion and or lack of history. "And where a prisoner hung himself!" As though that was the more powerful legend of the old jailhouse in modern Philadelphia.

In the back room there are heavy, gouged, leftover marks on floor and ceiling. I look out a back low wide window and see a thick iron jail door, rusted, setting up against a back wall. "Some man came here and bought that a year ago but never came back to pick it up. It's all that's left of the original jailhouse," she says.

Chelsea wonders aloud why the owners of the building had saved just that one cell door. Maybe the man bought it before they remodeled, years ago, and the owners of the building kept it while throwing everything else away? It stands haunting, weighted, and rusting against a back brick wall.

Belongs in a museum! I say. The woman remains silent, cordial.

We walk a couple blocks away from the old jail, now the Technical Appraisal Service Company, sightseeing, until Chelsea says she wants to get out of Philadelphia, that the air here is making her ill. I feel nauseous too. It's strange. The people we have met here have been very hospitable, within what is no doubt a complex traditional Southern condition, racism as complex as it gets, maybe even perfected; still, there's something else, unspoken, hovering . . . something very unsettling about this place. It's hard to explain.

We drive down 19. Turn right on 492 and I think about stopping a little southwest on 492 to take some pictures but don't. And continue driving and driving and Chelsea begins to screech that she can smell something dead in the outside air. I don't smell much; the windows are closed, the air conditioner is on. But I grow more and more silently terrified, watching, privately envisioning then and now, passing brand-new pickup trucks driven by red-faced white men, only white men, as the rain clouds grow more and more gray.

44 days later, in an earthen dam.

We drive a wide arc on Route 21 toward the Neshoba Fairgrounds and Old Jolly Farm where they were buried—Michael Schwerner, Andrew Goodman, and James Chaney, all together. Actually, we can't really decipher what was once Old Jolly Farm even in passing it, turning around and passing it again, so we stop across from the fairgrounds on 21, and I stand in front of a tree for a long time while Chelsea videotapes. I stand under a broad oak tree next to a red truck with its passenger-seat window completely covered with a Dixie flag. I am not wearing the Jimmie Rodgers T-shirt, and I don't think of moving, improvising, not at all, not to Jimmie Rodgers' music, his blues, nor anybody else's. My body is only capable of standing, that's all. I step out of our giant maroon Grand Marquis pimp car and stand in front of a tree. No one bothers us. And the sun appears from behind a cloud.

We complete the circle back to Philadelphia and drive down 19 once again, and I think about stopping a little southwest on 492, on Rock Cut Road, whatever road it might be called now, near where they were shot—Schwerner and Goodman once, Chaney six times—to take some pictures, but don't. And keep straight. Going fast but not speeding down 19. I tell Chelsea that I will never come to this place again.

We talk about how quaint Money was and how the Tallahatchie felt kind of "light," clean even, even with the deer-hunting bullets whizzing by, those timeless sonic echoes. Something benevolent had perhaps cleaned up the evil that had been there. And how Yazoo City seemed benign even with the hoards of white men hanging around, draped in camouflage and rebel flags. Clementine and Skip James's music were there.

We found no savior in Neshoba County. But maybe we weren't there long enough.

The next morning we drive to Hattiesburg. Stop and have lunch at a tiny diner, a sandwich shop right off the railroad tracks, one recently owned by a young retired serviceman. He had been to New York City one summer recently, said he didn't really consider New York City the North. "Massachusetts, that's North." He says to me that the one thing he didn't like about visiting New York City was the gender politics he picked up in the bars he visited. How the men there would not give up their seats for women in a crowded bar. And how, even with their dates, maybe wives, these same men would look conspicuously at any and all the women that would walk by. "If I ever did something like that, my wife would cut me up, probably kill me! It's wrong to act like that. That's the only thing I have against New York City."

We order turkey sandwiches, and I also ask for a book of matches and a glass of water. The owner brings the water and matches right away and goes back into his kitchen to prepare our sandwiches. I take the book of matches, open it, strike a match, and immediately place the lit match in the glass of water, extinguishing it. Could I get another glass of water? I ask, as the owner returns to the counter. "What happened to that one?" he asks, puzzled.

Oh, I wanted to put the fire out, I tell him.

During Freedom Summer in 1964, Hattiesburg led the state in Freedom School enrollment with six hundred elementary and high school–age children in classes held in local churches. That same summer, The Free Southern Theater, an experimental touring repertory company, gave performances in Hattiesburg of Samuel Beckett's *Waiting for Godot*. In 1966, the prominent African American businessman Vernon Dahmer, who had housed many of the activists during Freedom Summer, lost his life when his home was fire-bombed.

A Small World
Federal investigators believe Sam H. Bowers, the Imperial Wizard of the Ku Klux Klan, ordered the murder of Schwerner, also known as "Goatee." For Chaney and Goodman, their proximity to Schwerner was shitty (and heroic) timing. During the 1967 trial, Delmar Dennis, a self-confessed Klansman, said Bowers made his plan known in a coded letter about lumbering. Bowers received a ten-year sentence in 1967. He served no more than six years. In 1988, Bowers was convicted and sentenced to life in prison for the murder of Vernon Dahmer. (Bowers died in custody at the Central Mississippi Correction Facility near Pearl in 2006.)

ASSASSINS

.

BYRON DE LA BECKWITH

SHERIFF CECIL RAY PRICE

EDGAR RAY KILLEN

When one looks at a map of the South, the Delta could end in Natchez, Mississippi, or New Orleans, Louisiana. We choose New Orleans, once again. A good departure point, because from here there's nothing but water.

I read somewhere that James Baldwin's stepfather was a laborer and a preacher who fled New Orleans, calling it "a new-world Sodom and Gomorrah." He migrated north to New York City, Harlem.

Chelsea and I have a half-day in New Orleans before flying back home. Hungry and killing time, we find some decent gumbo and interview a parking-lot attendant about what he knows about the blues, an ageless black man who knows very little about the blues, says he wouldn't bet any money about what he knows. But that if I want to know about the Mardi Gras Indians, he is an expert.

What Was Always There Story (six months later)
May 2002

"You got to come along with me. You'll never find your way back if you don't and that's the truth."

We park our rental in front of the Blue Front Cafe and hop into Jimmy Holmes's white Ford F150. It's ten minutes past noon, and ninety-five-year-old Mr. Walter Carter is waiting.

Without a shortcut, we drive through a tangled landscape of dirt and graveled pig trails, under a canopy of live oaks, the road shaped by that filtered sunlight, sheltered green. And then the other Deep South of bare wooden bridges, rain-fed ponds, cotton-field railroad crossings. Way before, I imagine, for a long time, only wild fertile landscape. Then Antebellum. A battle-ground, then Reconstruction. The Deep South. A battleground. A growing national mythology continues. The Delta, specifically, hill country. The country and its old American secrets.

"Look at it! Comin' from the big city, bet you can't believe that there's still untouched country like this. And people live out here!" Jimmy drives, smiling. "Been a long while since I've been out this way."

Jimmy drives these narrow dirt roads as if not a stretch or bend has been forgotten. And, yes, people live out here, in this "untouched country." A giant working farm, a little lived-in shack, a little lived-in shack, a giant working farm, the unkempt hills and dense forest delta obliterating the difference.

Ninety-five-year-old Mr. Walter Carter, the oldest known resident of Bentonia, Mississippi, looks like he could be in his late sixties, a small man. He's waiting outside a simple brick house, in front of his screen door, dressed for an outing. A tan Homburg, a dark blue jacket, tan creased slacks, a yellow plaid shirt, and dark brown snakeskin cowboy boots. "Thirty-five minutes late," he barks.

After a few requisite photos in front of the house, a line up of Carter, his wife, and her three grinning grown-up nieces, we pile back into the truck and drive back to the Blue Front. Along the way, another point of view, Mr. Carter gives commentary on houses and yards of past friends and relatives, a yelling tour guide with perfect vision and almost deaf. "I've outlived everybody," he brightly bellows. The landscape changes colors, takes on Carter's history and remembering, becomes vernacular and mundane, all the way to the Blue Front.

Jimmy parks. Mr. Carter hops out of the truck and practically jogs to the porch of the café, anxiously waiting for Jimmy to unlock the door. "The pulse of this town," says Jimmy. "If it weren't for this place, there'd be no place, no town, and that's the truth."

We enter and sit in white plastic chairs, in the foreign afternoon darkness of the Blue Front. Jimmy offers us Cokes.

"Now, you've got to yell so he can hear you," Jimmy reminds me.

I had prepared a few simple questions for Mr. Carter. Sitting inches away from him, I yell so that he can hear.

So Mr. Carter, the oldest known resident of Bentonia, Mississippi! How does that make you feel?

"Don't know. All my friends are dead."

"He's got more energy then most folks I know," Jimmy shouts from behind the bar.

"I don't have much appetite, but I eat when I need to eat. Doctor gave me some medicine to make me hungry, cost fifteen dollars and didn't do nothin', fifteen dollars and didn't do nothin'."

I'm sorry to hear that, I say, and then I try again.

What makes you happy?

"Bein' around people, laughin' and talkin'. Jokin'. Lookin' at the TV. The soaps. *Guiding Light*'s my favorite."

How 'bout before? Do you remember or did you ever see *Amos and Andy*?

"That was good. I liked that show. You can't get no good ones on TV now, gotta have cable."

Were those characters very different from the people you knew, grew up with?

"No, not that much. I liked 'em."

How 'bout movies, what's your favorite movie?

"Don't watch movies. You need cable for that. All the good stuff's on cable."

I mean in a movie theater.

"Never been to a movie theater."

How 'bout music? What do you like to listen to?

"Oh, I like any music."

Did you ever play guitar?

"Oh boy, no!"

"He played with the women," Jimmy laughs.

Did you know Skip James? Jack Owens? Henry Stuckey?

"Yeah, yeah, I knew Skippy James. Skippy James. He was different from most folks. He was a preacher for while. Then he'd play music, then he'd preach. Made a couple records, two or three. Jack I knew, a musician too. He stayed right up the road here. Went across the water to play. He and I was almost the same age. Stuckey, a musician too. A fisherman, fished all the time, every day. Used to live right off 49. He would give a juke and we'd go to his place to frolic, when I was eighteen, nineteen, stay all night. He died over there in Satartia. They was all farmers."

Frolic?

"Frolickin', jukin', dancin', havin' a good time."

Jukin?

"Dancin'. The waltz . . . the one-step . . . two-step . . . the slow drag."

The one-step, the slow drag? Do you remember any of them?

"I don't know, it been so long. Well . . . yeah, I reckon so."

He gradually stands, unexpected, surprising everybody. Standing still for a few seconds, outside of remembering, and then he starts to move, mostly his legs, sliding, without bending any limbs, announcing and then moving from step to step. First the one-step, then the two-step, then the slow drag. His body thin as a rail and light, stiff, shining. Arms rounded. Hat tilted to the side. His cowboy boots scratching out music on the sandy concrete floor, surprising himself. Then he stops, places his hands on his chest, coughing, smiling, A revelation.

"Did you see that? See that rhythm his feet got? I didn't know he could do that," Jimmy shouts, clapping. "That's old, partner, that's old. I been knowin' him all my life and never known he could do that."

We are all clapping.

I ask if he would do the slow drag again, the side-step with the weird rhythm? It was remarkable. He demonstrates it again, a little puzzled this time, stepping and now forgetting. After a few seconds he stops and sits, crosses his arms, unfazed.

A train roars by, suspending the interview and time. Until Mr. Carter mentions something about a young boy in Jackson who lost his legs recently, playing too near the tracks. It confused him.

"I bet he crawled up under that thing while it wasn't runnin'," he says.

Jimmy nods.

The whistle seems to go on forever, a long freight; maybe five minutes goes by before I can ask my next question.

Did you ever have any problem with white people, a long time ago?

"No, not really. I know'd what you had to do to get along with them. You had to say 'yessir' and 'no sir.' You couldn't just say 'yes' and 'no.' You couldn't say you couldn't do what they asked. You had to try and do it."

Was that hard for you?

"Oh, yeah." He laughs. "It was hard."

Walter, do you remember the story of a man named Minnifield, who was lynched, burned at the stake, in Yazoo City around 1923? You would have been sixteen. All the black people in town supposedly fled, ran off. That would have been you and your family too.

"Minnifield? Minnifield . . . maybe I knew someone named Minnifield, sounds familiar. Maybe I heard something about it, but if I did I forgot it, been so long. I do know a man named Winfield, lives down the road."

He pauses. And uncrosses his arms.

"They hung Gary, hung him, when I was a chap. He was goin' with Miss Lilly Wallace, Gary was. Her husband was dead. Miss Taylor, her sister, stayed with her that night, with Miss Wallace, and saw Gary sneakin' by the window and turned him in. Because of the rain they tracked him. Brought him over to Captain Taylor's place. Captain Taylor told Gary if he told him the truth they wouldn't bother 'im. Gary told the truth and Captain hollered, 'Come and get 'im boys!' Gary was stupid, believin' Captain Taylor like that. 'Come and get 'im boys!' They hung him from an ol' plum tree, over there across the tracks that we chilluns used to play in. We called it Gator Limb, us chilluns, played up under it every day. That's why they hung him there, I believe. Big ol' tree set over side of the dirt road. They left him hangin' there till a white woman came down the road the next day, in a buggy and horse, and got scared, made the black folks take him down."

Was Lily Wallace a white woman?

"Yeah. She and Gary was goin' together. Secret."

Is the tree still there, the plum tree?

"Oh man, no! No, man, no! That was a long time ago."

What was Gary's last name?

"I don't remember."

Six months earlier, I had danced in the Blue Front. In between trying to decipher a music that I could not decode, practically stomping my feet, and restoring Buddy's empty beer bottles, I sat, if one could call it sitting, and waited for something fast, upbeat. It never came. What is left of the environment of the blues. What was always there. So I waited and then said, Fuck it, and didn't wait for an opportunity, for the music to say yes, come join us. I got up from my plastic chair and began to move to the song, a boisterous dirge, like the rest of the music. A dance that had no steps or shape, like the music. No longer research. I disappeared, rhythmically, without discrimination. But not in the way I had dreamed a few years back, conjure-dancing with Papa Satterwhite. There were no grandfathers or great-grandfathers ghosting this dance, no Frank Lafayette Satterwhite or blind William (Billy) Belk or W.I. Just me, barely me. I danced, with bended knees. A once-intelligent moving body breaking down onto a very hard floor while Jimmy and Buddy played "Hard Time Killin' Floor Blues," oblivious to my dancing, while the onlookers, smiling, sitting around tables that prop up untidy ash trays and cans of Budweiser, watched and nodded, acknowledging how my body was losing its opinion, in the bottomless soul of this place.

I stopped, sat down, no one clapped, no one said yes, nothing became more vivid, the music continued. And I was the only one surprised.

I remembered something Jimmy said. "Once, when those folks were shooting the Levi's commercial, one of the camera crew, a boy from England, somewhere like that, walked into the place and fell to his knees and wept, howling, that he'd heard of juke joints all his life but never thought he'd ever see a real one."

A few days after this experiment, I thought how presumptuous I had been, dancing there, trying to experience something, trying to make something happen, forcing a complex event, even though private and somewhat obscure in a place where there was absolutely no reason for obscurity, no discernible reason. Instead, what I found was perfect absence, a screaming dumb blankness, a complete refusal of the dance to occupy a space I could never understand, because it keeps changing. Very unpoetic, this realization.

And a perversity of fate, I yell.

Like the story of Gary, whose last name Mr. Carter couldn't remember, or maybe never knew. (Gary is now just Gary, and in the end that is his history.)

Mr. Carter, arms crossed, legs outstretched and crossed, continues to listen, if now showing a little exhaustion.

I then try to explain the particular absence I had experienced, without once using the word history. I also leave out the words dancing and dying, in an attempt to make a more spiritual point. Ultimately, Mr. Carter doesn't understand, or doesn't hear my queries, has nothing to say. He doesn't ask me to dance, again, so that he can see for himself.

And I have no more questions for him. We sit facing one another in silence, listening, like the rest of the Blue Front community, to R&B music from a jukebox that now blasts through the juke joint, until Mr. Carter falls asleep.

The pulse of the town? 6 a.m. to 10 p.m., normal hours, modern hours, and no dirt floor, not this time. The whole town does seem to wander in and out of the Blue Front—kids, teenagers, adult men, women, and seniors, except at night when it's mostly just men. All black, but for the occasional European or Japanese. This is not an all-black town, by the way, absolutely not.

After a few minutes Mr. Carter wakes and suddenly shares a story, as if he thinks I've asked another question, or as though it were a dream he just had, about a big, black, buzzard-like bird, a prophecy bird, that flew over his house when he was a small boy, a bird he'd never seen before and never saw again, and how the next day his uncle had his brains blown out with a shotgun. Mr. Carter, wide-awake now, then boasts about how he doesn't need a "stick" at ninety-five and how amazing that is. Says before he retired he was a gardener for a long time. Says he's been retired for a long time. Says he has to jog around his house every night, right before bed; otherwise he can't sleep.

An Incomplete Chronology II (and events I left out)

March 2001

Research event #1. St. Marks Danspace Benefit. New York City. First informal (dissemination) performance of research material to an audience outside of the South. (The first of twenty-four over two-and-a-half years.)

August 2001

Research event #3. Before moving forward with any "theatrical" questions about some of my visits to the South, I conduct a workshop to revisit Geography, the very beginning of the trilogy material at Virginia Commonwealth University, with Kouakou Yao "Angelo," Djédjé Djédjé Gervais, and Goulei Tchépoho. I think it would be good to start from the beginning. It is a failure. Angelo is no longer interested in this kind of exploration. He has a job in a hotel in Vermont, a SUV, and a nice apartment. And I discover I no longer need Goulei's Djembe, that percussion and energy, that kind of nudging, not like before. Djédjé and I continue working together.

November 2001

The "Dancing/Dying tour." Travel through the "Mississippi Delta/The Living Room Dances" (for family and friends of Frank Stokes, Mississippi Fred Mcdowell, Robert Johnson, and Skip James) and more Lynching Site Counter-Memorials (Emmett Till, Willie Minnifield, Chaney, Goodman and Schwerner, Vernon Dahmer).

January 2002

Second trip to Sapelo Island, Georgia, with Katherine Profeta, David Thomson, Djédjé Djédjé Gervais, and Chelsea Lemon Fetzer. A search and transmission of the Buzzard Lope, a nineteenth-century Ring Shout dance, from centenarian, Hicks Walker. I also perform/document the Boneyard event in the Atlantic ocean to an audience of fallen skeletal trees. Facing away from Africa, waist high in water, I read excerpts from Arne Bontemps's "A Summer Tragedy."

March 2002

A private "Living Room Dance," transported to an informal event audience environment, the UCLA World Arts and Cultures students and faculty, for Bruce Langhorne, the black guitarist who played on seminal early Bob Dylan recordings, "A Hard Rain's Gonna Fall," etc. Stuff I've been listening to since I was a teenager.

(Fleeting Almost Illusionary)

Ah, the Dylan dance! A live experiment with unreliable certainty.

I was certain that Dylan didn't write "Don't Think Twice . . ." via some emotional but sketchy research. I assumed it was an old blues song, composed by some unknown Mississippi master. I was also certain that Langhorne played guitar on the original Dylan recording; it even says so in the liner notes of the CD I own, *The Freewheelin' Bob Dylan*.

So, I invited Langhorne, who lives in Los Angeles, to UCLA, where I was in residence, so that I could dance for him, to the original "Don't Think Twice It's Alright." Him playing guitar forty years ago, on an old blues song sung by Dylan. What a great confluence, and a public one, on now and then and who's who, right?

Well . . .

This is an email from Langhorne after my dance, after all the applause:

Hi Ralph,

Nice meeting you and experiencing your work first hand. Sorry, the erroneous liner notes gave me a credit, which I didn't deserve. I don't like to take credit for anyone else's work (even though that is the way of the world). I hope that I didn't cause you any embarrassment.

Bruce

It was Dylan who played guitar on "Don't Think Twice It's Alright" and Langhorne also later recalled that Dylan did indeed write the song. He was there.

So, three truths:

1. It is not an old black song.

2. My performance was absolutely perfectly fake.

3. Who the fuck is Bob Dylan?

Race and Backyards Redux
The summer before I met 95-year-old Mr. Walter Carter
July 2002
A family of four, a father, mother, and two small boys, not yet teens, dressed head to toe in hunting camouflage, sat at a Shoney's banquette on the afternoon of the Fourth of July. The mother, sitting across from the silent and erect father, placed her head in her arms and collapsed forward unto the table, sobbing. The small boys watched, uncertain, waiting cautiously for whatever else was to follow, including their hamburgers.

I mentioned the above story to a sometimes-intelligent white friend who commented: *"Trash* in the dictionary is *worthless stuff. White trash* is the racial equivalent of *nigger,* but not really. White trash refers to poor white folk who don't have the economic power to look down on other worthless folk. They are also an embarrassment to well-off white folk cause they make poor black folk just poor folk and not poor fucked-up black niggers. White trash are the great equalizers of our racist society. They also tend to be as racist if not more than their better-off Caucasoid brothers and sisters. Not to be confused with *rednecks* who are a different breed altogether. Rednecks being the difference. I've never heard the term Black trash, or poor Black trash. White trash also tend to be very overweight, are in a choice-less love with processed foods. Just like poor black folks. Now *niggers* are something completely different. I know it meant one thing once, but now *nigger* is heterogeneous, and becoming more and more an attitude, like *nigga*s, for instance. This attitude is not necessarily based on economics nor is it based on being fat. And then there are simply black people, who also have little pretense in public."

You're kind of full of shit, I tell her, but think to myself:

Trinity
"Black people like Jesus and fried chicken."

Weather
"It's sticky as shit out here."

Post Office
"Let me see that . . ."
"Why's he pink? Must be some rock 'n' roll musician."
"You wouldn't buy that stamp if you didn't know who he was."
"I wouldn't buy it, unh, unh, he's ugly!"
"Yeah, you're only maybe gonna buy this stamp if you know who Andy Warhol is."

I'm next in line, behind the Warhol stamp conversation. What a great title for something, *Who Andy Warhol Is,* I'm thinking. I buy a whole page of the Warhol stamps. The stamp looks odd to me too but not as odd as the look I get from the woman behind the counter as she hands me my change.

Who Furry Lewis Is (to Arthur Lee)
"Why you lookin' for Furry Lewis? He was no link to the blues, not to B. B. King, not even to Elvis.

"I took one photograph of him . . . while he was drunk . . . He was mean to my assistant.

"I don't believe in showing work, making work that doesn't 'uplift,' so I don't have any photos of Furry.

"Never heard him sing Casey Jones, or anything. I don't like the blues, was never a blues fan. I'm just a photographer, I document.

"I like church music, that's the music I listen to."

I thought of asking Earnest Withers, a famous Memphis photographer, if he had heard of Arthur Lee, leader of the sixties LA rock band Love, who was born in Memphis, but then thought it would be a waste of time.
I saw Arthur Lee and Love live in Minneapolis, in 1970, when I was seventeen. At the time I couldn't imagine him being from the South.

Migration
My great uncle Homer used to be a chauffeur. He would sometimes borrow the old '46 Cadillac from his employer. He would drive his wife, Ruth, around. Aunt Ruth would sit in the backseat while Homer drove. This is when they lived in Indiana. His boss moved to Indiana from Macon, Georgia. They moved with him.

Another Homer, my dear friend Homer Avila, is a dancer. He just recently lost a leg and a hip to a rare form of cancer. At his apartment, hours before the surgery, he taped strips of masking tape to the leg to be amputated and then wrote on the tape with a blue magic marker, TAKE THIS ONE. NOT THE OTHER LEG, PLEASE.

A few months after the surgery Homer became famous and seems to dance and travel more on one leg than when he had both.

In later years James Baldwin considered himself a "commuter." "That was the only way I could've played it. I would've been broken otherwise. I had to say, 'A curse on both your houses.'"

The Engine Wiper
The Casey Jones Museum in Vaughan, Mississippi, is located near the site of the train wreck that took the life of the legendary engineer.

On April 30, 1900, the Cannonball left Memphis with Jonathan Luther Casey Jones. The tale of the ill-fated train would have ended on that April night had it not been for a friend of Jones and the popularity of vaudeville.

Walker "Wash" Saunders, a black engine wiper in Water Valley, and a friend of Jones, was deeply moved by Jones's death and wrote the song "The Ballad of Casey Jones." The song found its way to vaudeville and became a hit and Jones a legend. Saunders disappeared.

I dance to Furry Lewis's version of "The Ballad of Casey Jones" for two years straight, the Furry Lewis dance, I call it, never a "Living Room Dance." (I was never able to track down any of Furry's family members.) A concluding performance offering for my other and more familiar audience, outside of the South, in whatever small theater was offered, always after a recording of Frank Stokes or Bob Dylan or whoever else I'm thinking and dancing about out loud.

Besides Bessie Smith

Quite a few ageless, mostly black men sit in front of Jimmy "Duck" Holmes's brother's corner convenience store in downtown Bentonia.

"Where's Duck?"

Cell phones appear. Jimmy's brother is the first to connect, "He's at the school teaching today." He then calls out to a young girl, a name I can't decipher, his daughter. He asks her to lead, guide us to the school. This happens a lot around here, the leading, guiding part, their car, our car. Everyone drives.

Duck is at the school, somewhere. "He's in class right now. He's available mornings, before class . . . try then," an elderly receptionist says and guides us back out the school door. Duck's brother's daughter, I wish I knew her name, who's been waiting in the parking lot, leads us back to the highway. "Tell Duck I'll come back tonight," I wave. She nods and drives off in a different direction. In fifteen minutes we are back in Yazoo City.

Later that evening I drive back to Bentonia alone, to the Blue Front, leaving Chelsea at the motel. It's still padlocked. There are now more bodies of various genders and generations sitting, arriving, in front of Duck's brother's store. The store itself is also closed.

Cell phones appear. "He's at home." Another young girl is politely ordered to lead me to Duck's farm.

Hey Duck, remember me?

"Yeah, got your message but it was not so clear, lots of static."

My cell-phone service, sorry 'bout that.

It's good to see Jimmy "Duck" Holmes again. We talk for a few hours about how his father bought 130 acres for $9,000 in '44 or '47, how that was like a "million dollars then. He had saved it sharecropping. Died at age sixty-six . . . worked too hard. No, drank too hard."

Duck told me that his dad grew cotton on the 130 acres.

"Kids, rural kids, couldn't go to school until October, harvesting farmland. The school system understood this, that the rural kids, the farms were crucial to the economy. On rainy days they would go to school, but only half days. There was always something to do."

Duck excused himself for being "country." He was building a foundation for a tool shed the whole while we talked. And kept assuring me he was "listening."

"There's moccasin in the pond over there and no fish," he said.

"That little shotgun house there," falling apart on his property, "used to house the man who taught Skip James how to play."

Yes, I say, Henry Stuckey. I remember from the time before. You gave me a tour.

"Kids today don't care about the blues."

He then asks, "When you leaving?"

Tomorrow.

"You should drive down to Belzoni to see Paul Turner . . . missed his calling. What a voice. Guess he decided he didn't want to be B. B. King. Yep, guess not. That takes determination."

I don't know, maybe it's the moccasin in the lake . . . or that Chelsea's back at the motel, but I'm suddenly provoked to ask, without any noticeable provocation, other than the two of us standing in his backyard . . . Well, what about a woman? Do you know of any women that sing the blues around here?

"Nope."

Besides Bessie Smith and Memphis Minnie
Helen Kent, daughter of Frank Stokes, cradles her pistol in her tiny lap. "There was a woman, a neighbor, and a man broke into her house, came into her bedroom. She had been sewing the night before, so her scissors were near at hand and with the scissors she kept the man away until she got to her pillow where she kept her gun. Shot him dead. He told her he was gonna kill her but she got to him before he got to her. I guess it was a miracle that she had been sewin' the night before.

"I keep a gun near my bed, not under the pillow . . . in a drawer of the nightstand. Somebody break into my house, I won't miss, I betcha that. I shoot it every New Year's Eve, go in the back-yard and fire it in the air with all the other fireworks."

Jessie Mae Hemphill keeps her pistol in her tan 1985 Cadillac.

"I couldn't carry you with me, but I gotcha now," she recalled lovingly, describing her delight upon retrieving the gun, after a cargo plane carried her car from San Francisco to New York City then to London and Paris, while she performed her brand of North Mississippi hill coun-try blues and gospel.

When she was nine she had a boyfriend; he was sixteen. One time he brought a seventeen-year-old girl with him when he came to visit. Jessie Mae told him never to do that again. He did. And she took her mother's gun, which was lying on a table, "smack dab" between a Bible and a dictionary. She shot at her boyfriend and the girl five times, "emptied out the gun, as many bullets as there was. I boomed them some, had to. Didn't know how to shoot then. Every time I shot, my arm would fly up and behind my head. That was dangerous. If they had shot back I'd been kilt . . . my arm dangling behind my head every time I shot . . . Later, my aunt taught me how to bull's-eye.

"They ran off, over the hill, his hat flyin'. The girl broke a heel off her shoe, now that was funny. He never came back after that . . .

"I went back in the house and cleaned the gun, took a long stick and a piece of cloth, dipped it in kerosene, cleaned inside the barrel of the gun . . . put it back right where it was, between the Bible and the dictionary. My momma woulda kilt me, yes she would have. She died not knowin'.

"I was nine years old. Now, I ask you, how did a baby know how to clean a gun?"

At this point in the story Jessie Mae, still wearing her leopard-print Stetson hat, eases out of her blue velour recliner and grabs a brown rubber pail sitting nearby, lifts her yellow floral dress and places the pail under her bottom, squats . . . and Chelsea turns off the video camera.

Better Than Hip Hop
Clementine Davis connects us to Mr. Neal Roberts, a recreational therapist at St. Francis, a school and community center. A track star, injured and "left on the sidelines" by his coach. His work here is his "retaliation." He thinks of youth violence as "unfocused energy." "I try to wear them out for two hours after school. They go home refreshed."

Mexicans Have Their Mariachi
We pull off the road and stop alongside a vast and blooming cotton field in Bentonia. It's a month away from harvest. A red truck pulls off the road next to our car. An excited man jumps out and begins talking to himself and then us; about how soon he'll be busy making money at the cotton gin. He fingers a few plants, almost sexually, "Yeah, soon they'll be foliating the leaves."

There's a gin nearby. The man offers to lead us there. He does, but drives so fast that we lose sight of him along the way. The gin becomes obvious in the distance.

The ginner on hand is a Mexican, Hector.

"No, gin up norte?" He asks.

I have no idea, I say. Is there cotton in Mexico?

"Yeah, Sonora. I worked there. Now work here. Good, good to make money, buy food, some beer, a truck."

Hector spares me any embarrassment by not knowing or not mentioning cotton's pre-historic beginnings in Mexico.

The Japanese on the other hand . . .

I remember asking Asako, what do you think about when you think about the blues?

"Hmm, I sent CD for my parent's birthday. My father asked me to send a CD of anybody who are playing 'Sunny Side of the Street.' I sent 1930 recording of Billy Holiday. It didn't have 'Sunny Side of the Street' on it. He said he loved it. In his letter he wrote that he pulled the curtain, made the room a little dark, and listened to 'Strange Fruit,' again and again, between drawing, between housework. He'd go back to the room and listen. He also said he wish he has somebody to share that with. He doesn't know what she's singing, the lyrics. But Billy Holiday's singing evoke something in my father's heart. As I read his letter, many feelings, memories came back and squeezed me. Is that the blues?"

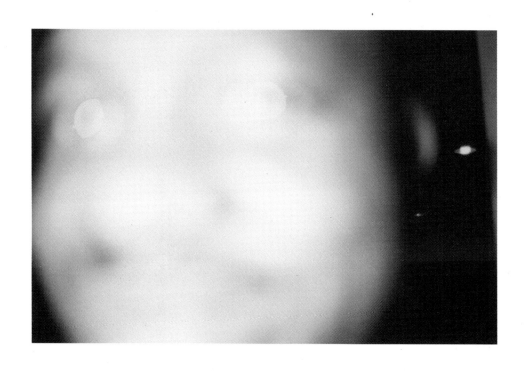

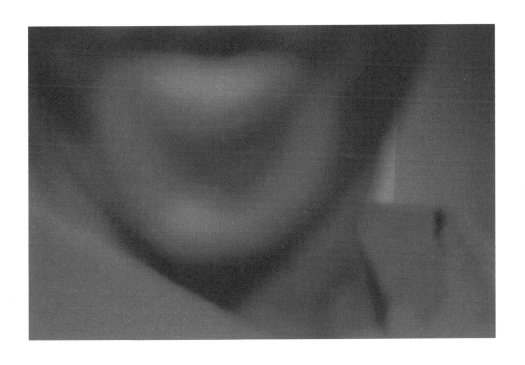

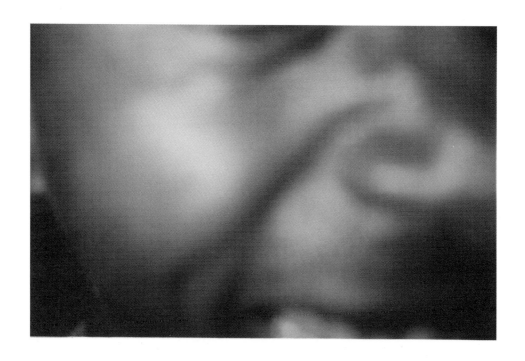

Process Repetition I
Or, how we begin to make theater with ghosts who have the blues

July 2002
Re: Remembering Birmingham. Walker Art Center residency.
Dear El,
Yeah, . . . a demonstration first would be great, and then I'd like to ask the police officer to experiment, very simply, within some choreography, i.e., the officer and dog would stand at one end of the stage and every time a dancer would get to a certain SAFE position near them the dog would try to attack. My hope is to incorporate this situation into a final performance in fall 2004. Every tour site/city would provide an officer and dog via the yet to be scored Minneapolis instructions. That's the idea. One day for a few hours with the officer and dog should be enough. If we do a showing at the end of the residency, and this experiment works, it'd be great to have them be a part of that.

Re: Re: Remembering Birmingham. Walker Art Center residency.
Hey Ralph,
I need to know more information about the context for what you want the dog and trainer for—people who do this work are very sensitive about using the word "attack" and they are really concerned about perpetuating negative stereotypes of dogs—so I'm dealing with a lot of suspicion.

Below is an excerpt of an email from a potential trainer:
"First, I don't have or know anyone that has 'attack' dogs. My dogs are sport dogs, just like a hunting dog, agility dog, etc. If I were to be involved, I would need to know the reason/purpose behind this request. I would never be involved in anything that perpetuated the negative stereotype of dogs in general or specific breeds."

Can you please give me some information so I can answer to these concerns? I am having much more luck with trainers who do Schutzhund work than with the police canine unit. Does it matter what kind of dog? Does it matter that it's not a cop? The Schutzhund training is exactly the same training as the police canine dogs do—it is done as a form of dog training sport.
Lemme know
Thanks—El

You can't always get what you want. Next time maybe. Anyway, the Walker has been very supportive, providing a mini production residency when I'm years away from a production. Quite luxurious and a two-week crash course on everything I've been thinking about lately. Bebe Miller's presence was superbly interesting, though she could only stay a week. Chelsea is videoing everything. Some great documented seeds to plant elsewhere. We have a pedal steel guitar player joining us on Thursday. But, as of yet, no attack dog. We've done some pretty interesting experiments anyway.

I've peed in a cup that Bebe balanced on her head to Miles Davis's *Porgy and Bess*.

David and Djédjé are now Amos and Andy, lip-syncing to Nina Simone.

Djédjé has an exercise where he dances with a live mic bouncing about in his pants.

Black black David does a standup skit about being "mixed race." He's serious. And it's very funny.

Djédjé plays horseshoes with a suspended basketball hoop.

David and Djédjé have a duet based on how they're the same black man. Djédjé made a beautiful simple solo sketch about lynchings that I could never have made.

Djédjé and I dance to Frank Stokes, "King of the Memphis Blues."

David's transcribing a "Bojangles" stair dance I made on the staircase outside the old Sapelo Island dance hall.

I made a study about the famous Madison Square Gardens Ali/Frasier fight. Pummeling myself.

Later David joins me with a hambone rhythm, slapping his body and thighs, eventually singing a doo-whop melody. This study most likely won't survive due to the painfulness of my self-pummeling.

All this stuff is directed within a certain proposition of absurdity (like most race issues and racism and what might be fundamental about minstrelsy). We'll see what lasts, transcends this guerilla-style process.

.

A LESS OBSTRUCTED VIEW

Desolation Row

We take a weekend off to visit Duluth, a beautiful city right on Lake Superior. The infamous lynching site, the one that Dylan sang about, is in a derelict part of town, so our "memorials" to Issac McGhie, Elmer Jackson, and Elias Clayton are aptly situated. We ramble around a yellow street-light pole, in all sincerity. I choose Elias Clayton, the last to fall, on an early Sunday morning, drunks and prostitutes as audience.

I ask Chelsea to circle me with the camera as I trip up Second Avenue, like maybe Elias—bumping into walls and cars, falling when it seems appropriate.

Reaching the stoplight, the yellow street-light pole, I press the red button to bring on the walk light. Waiting, circling the pole, quiet, leaning up against the wall of the old Shriners building looking at the new yellow, red, green pole.

I pick up a pebble, toss it in the air, sit, look up, stand. I lie down on my back on the sidewalk for a long time, thinking about the drunks across the street at the corner bar looking at me. Lying on the ground I could have been any of them, Issac or Elmer or Elias. Hard to tell from the old blurry photograph; three bodies in dungarees and overalls, with white shirts torn off, tied and twisted around their waists.

One body with his hands seemingly tied behind his back.

Another body with his hands bound in front of his body.

Two of the bodies are hanging from a street light or telephone pole with horribly stretched necks.

One body lies in front of the pole, lying face down, head turned to the right, arms free.

All seem to be wearing their shoes, boots, or at least one shoe, boot.

Drunks are up early drinking Gatorade outside the Kozy bar.

"What's that man doing on the corner? He's doing some weird shit!" one says.

Then David and Djédjé take turns. They both take off their shirts, both after about three minutes into their seven-to-ten-minute events. When Djédjé finishes, he walks across the street to the drunks and explains to them what it is he's doing.

"There's nothing you can do to change what happened, so in my mind I reached out to them . . . memorials are about healing."

The drunks are even more confused.

Another memory, history that has mostly disappeared from what is today. There were probably more black people in Duluth then than now. Now, there just seemed to be us. But actually:

"Back when the Kozy Bar still looked out on an empty lot, few people here knew what had happened to those men: three black circus workers who were hanged from a light pole on June 15, 1920, as a crowd of 10,000 looked on. Many white people had never heard of the lynching; older generations had chosen not to pass the memory down. Many African-Americans here— just 1,415 black people are counted among the population of 86,000—had heard of it, but spoke about it quietly, among themselves." December 4, 2003, Monica Davey for the *New York Times*.

Back in Minneapolis, at the Walker, we make a dance called Duluth using these keywords:
Walk
Press a button
Make circle
Back against a wall
Look up
Pick up a coin lying on the ground
Toss it in the air
Lie on your back
Reorder as you wish

Warning
Very little of what happened at the Walker workshop will make it into a final performance work two years later. Duluth does, especially Elias. Nina Simone does, and the horseshoes and the basketball hoop continue. Miles Davis, Frank Stokes, Bojangles, Amos and Andy, Mohammed Ali and Joe Frasier don't. Neither does Bebe Miller and the urine. (The process can't really afford Bebe Miller, partly due to the fact that she's too famous.)

Some Pretty Loud Thinking
This workshop has been an opportunity to bring my "It is what it is" research to one of my classical "Hinting at references" playpens. Bold ambiguity versus actually and artfully describing the thing itself. An aesthetization of discursive certainty, perhaps. Whatever it is, it is my karma. All the (few) workshops thus far are also contentious reactions. Seems necessary for now. A good thing to try to articulate.

At the moment I'm reacting to how very little of my inordinate research seems to be about the stage, as I know it. And so far, there's not a glimmer of how I might translate it. In fact, and this is very interesting, I don't think I want this research to be about the stage, where it has to become, at best, relevantly artificial. But not exactly.
These studio questions may or may not be valid:
No theatrical black vernacular! Why?
Why would it not be necessary to experiment with cultural clichés?
Would it be as unnecessary, reacting to modern theatrical forms?
Is my dance form dead? If so, then what?
Is it old-fashioned? If so, then what?
How does one push an older body? Older bodies?
How to make a private experience theatrical and innovative?

William Isom Satterwhite, Aunt Mattie, Malcom X, the American South, the blues have been essential improvisational elements to my research practice and to my thinking about being a theater artist. But here, in Process Repetition I, where I get to formally deflect meaning, Aunt Mattie and the rest are of peripheral interest, a personal, if haphazard, resource to my working with traditional performing artists in a traditional theater (versus a private solo event in a graveyard or ocean or living room). This may be my undoing but the data is there, my equivalency testing, my twelve (so far) informal research dissemination events in front of a small but select theater audience, have shown me that I'm not much interested in imposing any discovered and direct black Southern bluesy Americanness to a modern art–theater audience. I think it would be a failure, too out of context. What I have put on stage informally and what I do ultimately put on a larger stage, at some arbitrary date, after spending some four stretched-out years, in a black Southern bluesy America, is anybody's guess, a random guess.

At the moment, what interests me in this conventionally enclosed workshop is what is theatrically contradictory about what the Freedom Bus Ride meant/means to all black Americans and David Thomson's elegant bathing habits (for example: "a communion with the waters of life, a healing refuge at the end of the day").

So yeah, I'm moving onward from what's come before, but of course, also not. I'm discovering that there are, for me, many important undecipherable connections to be had in the elusive memory architecture of Robert Johnson's proposed third gravesite near Money. Or to the charming placement of the Edmund Pettus Bridge in Selma. And to the leftover concrete foundation that lies in front of a freshly painted white tract house that used to support the trailer home of Mississippi Fred Mcdowell. Unreliable memory foundations, built to last centuries. (Or twenty to thirty years at most.)

The Last Family Goat Barbeque Picnic Story

It's the end of August 2002. Clyde Brown, Ruby Brown's father, leads us in his 1970 tan Chevrolet pickup from Como to Gavel Springs, driving exactly thirty miles an hour the whole way, to Otha Turner's backyard Family Goat Barbeque Picnic on Labor Day weekend. "With dancing and foot-stompin' music you ain't gone see or hear nowhere else."

It is the beginning of the party, about 5 p.m., and the farm is busy with mostly white middle-aged men, helping Otha and his family get things ready, hanging light fixtures, boiling goat meat; the goat is quartered, almost everything is used.

More, younger, white couples show up, some with guitar cases. All from out of town, Memphis, Nashville, Amsterdam, Japan.

As soon as it gets dark, the black nearby community arrives.

RL Boyce thumps a chord or two, occasionally, perfect, essential, even when he's too drunk to continue, or to climb onto the stage to try again. He orders a young white man onto the stage to take over, Luther Dickinson, a student of RL, so says RL. RL says, "This one is on to greatness." He is already famous, this one.

Ah, the dancing. Barefoot, the blacks. And if there's a woman of any color around she's being humped. If she's white she smiles, embarrassed. If she's black she humps back, and I wouldn't call it a smile. I don't see anything resembling what I imagine as a buck dance, and can't imagine this is "how they used to do it." Or what Ruby saw when she was a little girl, right here, and Ruby's not around to ask. One thing's for sure, none of my "Living Room Dances" looked like this.

There are B-B-Q goat sandwiches and canned beer for sale. Many bring their own brew, disguised in plastic cups, indiscernible, what it is. Whatever the hell it is.

In the pitch, everyone is really drunk now.

RL climbs back onto the stage and, holding the microphone for dear life, screams, "I'm gwine . . . I'm gwine . . ." over and over again, a drum and guitar accompanying the repetition.

The music is at it's best when it's at its sloppiest. While white young men play audibly sharp . . . clear, like good and sometimes exceptional students.

Otha Turner appears and disappears, occasionally leading his family, marching, drumming, with his fife, this blues-martial music from the nineteenth-century military tradition, via Africa. It is the glue to the proceedings . . . and why perhaps no one seems afraid.

"Saturday night is the night everybody shows up." Tomorrow. Near the end of this night, there are more black folk than white, more men than women.

At the end of the night RL Boyce gives me his card and asks if we're coming again tomorrow.

Maybe we could pick him up in Como and drive over together, so we don't get lost. He said he'd like to leave his house late, "avoid the heat of the day."

Saturday, early evening, we drive to Como looking for RL's house, "The white one, 103 Sicamore, the house just around the corner." We drive along Sicamore and then around Sicamore for 45 minutes, looking for the white house. And then we decide to drive to Otha's farm on our own.

We drive a few miles toward Senatobia on some backroads that look a lot like the roads we drove following Mr. Brown the day before. But we're lost. We stop at a house and ask a group of people sitting in the front yard, "Do you know RL?"

"Yep, he's in the house. Come on in," says a smiling woman sitting on the front steps.

"No, he's not here," shouts another voice from inside the house. "He's at Otha's."

Thank you very much, I say, incredulous, and we drive off.

Gravel Springs. RL is already at the picnic, already drunk. Once again explaining to me how he "learnt" all the young white guys how to play the blues. Some he "learnt just a little."

It's early, 6 p.m., and the farm is filled with mostly a large crowd of white people sitting around in lawn chairs, ready for some entertainment.

Chelsea and I make a bet on what time the demographics will shift, "8, 9, 10 p.m.?" It's a silly bet of course. It all depends on when the sun goes down.

The sun sets around eight and the black community reclaims the farm. And white groups also continue to show up. One group is uniformed; baseball hats, T-shirts, khaki pants, a giant beer cooler, and two young women with blonde hair, one wearing a straw cowboy hat. This group seems the most out of place. They plop their cooler right in the center of the crowd, right in front of the stage, oblivious, their dusty decorum, impervious to who may have been there before, their jerky dancing taking over, hee-hawin'. And not a single person of the hundreds of people there laughs at them.

There is them and there is a young man, nineteen, from North Carolina. "There's no blues in Raleigh, so I'm stayin' with Otha," he tells me. His mother was also there, his chaperone. I doubt she was also staying with Otha. She must have had a motel room somewhere in Senatobia. She's very proud. "Ain't he amazin'? Can play piano, drums, guitar, and he's so young. Gonna be good someday." He is ambitious, that's for sure. Is on stage whenever no one else wants to be.

Richard Johnston (Memphis street and studio musician) and Luther Dickinson (of the Mississippi Allstars) occasionally play but have to be coaxed. These young men play the blues precise and clean and adventurous, and loud. The older black guys play drunk, the music constantly falling apart, interrupted and vitally static, as though they get stuck on one thought and then forget that they are thinking, or get bored, passing the microphone or guitar on to someone else . . .

On this night there are no young black men playing music, precise or broken. There are black women that come to the stage to stomp and sing but not to play any instruments, and there are no young black boys or girls on the stage doing anything other than tussling with each other and or dancing.

But the stage is shared happily, intoxicatingly with whoever needs to be there, to sing, or dance, or play guitar or drums, out of body. They don't care. The music is another way to stagger, to walk, and one always needs to walk, even if wobbly, to get away.

North Mississippi hill country blues is slow and certain, a specific "country" sound, without rural boundaries. Its nature is to fall apart, before a song is finished. Sometimes, most times, it stops without preparation or purpose, just stops, because it has to. Another chord begins. Stops. There are constant interruptions.

Idea: The blues was developed in a state of inebriation, real and metaphoric, affecting, shaping its sound and evolving culture.

The music is not precious. Getting drunk and partying, dancing, remembering that one can grab a guitar or the microphone, if one wants, is perhaps more precious. Perhaps.

A visitor may be challenged with this paradox, that the local black audience loves this music but ultimately doesn't care about its survival. There's always some other entertainment. Nothing lasts long enough to cherish. There is no real distinction between stage and performer, between when the music is there and when it's not.

When it's there you dance. When it's not you do something else. And one can always dance.

Otha appears and disappears, periodically, leads his Rising Star Fife and Drum Band, his family, through the crowd, while also signing autographs or chaperoning Shardé Thomas, his thirteen-year-old fife protégé, who's also a fierce drummer. Otha uses what energy he has left in three-minute riffs. Sometimes the riffs last as long as four minutes.

Shardé is in a bad mood tonight, or so it seems. She is constantly congratulated, comprehending little of what it all means, just like her grandfather.

Around 11 p.m. Otha seems to tire and for the remainder of the evening can be found sitting on an old rickety bench, shadowed under a young oak tree, peacefully asleep.

In the middle of one of the last precarious sets, a young white man looks at me, smiles, and says, "Isn't this amazing!?" I nod, and walk away from the front of the stage where I've been sitting, away from the young man and the three older black men hammering out chords and changing their minds, passing the only guitar, the last one of the night, back and forth, or singing into an unamplified microphone, or laughing, hopping.

"Amazing!?" Yes, of course. What an exotic scene and how curious and entertaining, inscrutable, harmless. And easy to love.

Near the end of the night there are reports that there are fights out on the road. Where the younger, hipper, Gravel Springs black community listens to hip hop in and around their vehicles, finding the picnic too old-fashioned but still worth congregating nearby. The police arrive and order the music of the picnic stopped. It doesn't, and continues to die, on its own terms, like before.

And from this death, dying, I return home, again, and begin to think about making something, in earnest, doing something more practical and less apparitional, wondrous, with all this watching and listening and taking notes. Returning this time almost exclusively back to the world of modern cities, those in authority, with durable architectonic theaters and stages. Also back to the necessary fiction of my left brain. Continuing a research more urban and migrated, in all sorts of ways. I also need to find my twenty-first-century body again.

"Now why would you have to do that?" RL Boyce asks, in the pitch dark.

Well, for the moment, after being down here, back and forth for a year and four months, I just can't imagine myself living in Mississippi, I tell him.

ART MAKE-UP , NO . 3: GREEN

Process Repetition II
More notes on the twentieth century

September 2002
I watch a pirated video of Bruce Nauman's 1964–65 *Wall-Floor Positions* for first time.

Letter to Bruce Nauman's Studio
There is much I could say about this request, there are many layers, but I'll try to keep it simple.

I first saw *Wall-Floor Positions* at the Whitney Biennial, what, eight years ago? I was "floored." I've been experimenting with movement for most of my life and viewing this performance/ body work/film/video stunned most of what thought I knew about moving. I did some research and discovered that Nauman did indeed make "dances," sort of.

Nauman's "dances" from the sixties are fascinating to me for their commitment and rigor to an "amateur" movement/art/dance perspective, the simplicity and obvious commitment to the task, and in how they differ from the work of the Judson Church dance canon, "postmodern dance," of the same period. That his "dances" surfaced to be more about being human (and untrained) than about anything else.

And there was/is the important time placement of these works. If my reading serves me correctly, Nauman created a version of *Wall-Floor Positions* in 1965(?), the same year Congress passed the Voting Rights Act and the same year Trisha Brown created *Homemade*, a seminal postmodern dance work. The 1968 film version of *Wall-Floor Positions* was made the year of Martin Luther King Jr.'s assassination. These seemingly disparate events are a defining and fraught part of my history as an artist and racial being.

What specifically interests me about *Wall-Floor Positions* beyond it's obvious relationship to art and the body, the beautifully ordinary and rigorous movement statement that it is, is the not so obvious parallel realities of a period in time, of "a white art freedom" and the black civil rights movement. Body as art material (I would posit that at the time Nauman embodied this concept/movement gloriously). And the body as invisible chattel. Where and how did these forces intersect beyond an inanimate sociology of walls and floors? Was that possible? Does it matter? The proximity of these things is of course precarious.

My partner in this potential venture is Djédjé Djédjé Gervais, a dance artist from Coté d'Ivoire, West Africa. I've been collaborating with Djédjé since 1997. Since our first meeting, our bodies have taken on some very interesting and useful ideas about American "modernity" as tradition, and West African "tradition" as something always modern. We are coming to separate but equal, simple terms. I could go on but won't.

My hope is that Nauman will send us detailed instructions to the original work, or new instructions that we would then follow. Our plan and participation in this "re-creation," is to place our physical history and body art politics in what I feel is a historically major movement work about a body negotiating a wall and a floor. In how that work is representative of now, and perhaps what it represented then. And it would be a "re-creation," not a "translation." Of course Djédjé and I bring different bodies, training, understandings, (unstable) cultures, and time elements to what Nauman originally intended—all the better. After all, it's 2002, not 1965/68. Nevertheless, it will essentially remain what Nauman structured. That is my hope.

My only request, beyond permission to recreate *Wall-Floor Positions*, is to have a free-standing wall so that Djédjé and I could perform the work simultaneous on either side of the wall, holding a conversation with Nauman's intended wall and floor, and with each other. Nauman, if it interests him, could also newly structure what this "simultaneity" is/should be.

As far as crediting the performance, we would be performing a "Nauman" work. Unless there's a more specific credit Nauman desires.

Let me know if I've left anything out. Thank you. R

What May Have Been Left Out Story
January 7, 2003
"She's not well but says she can't wait to meet you," Yolanda says over the phone, from an office in the basement of the Museum of Contemporary Art in Chicago. "She says you sound like an interesting man with an interesting project. Yes, an interview will be fine . . . She's still haunted by the story and still needs to repeat it, word for word. 'People need to be aware,' she's always saying. You know, she founded her own theater group called The Emmett Till Players, a youth theater group that produces civil rights–themed plays here in Chicago."

Mamie Till-Mobley's father moved his family to Chicago from Webb, Mississippi, just after she was born, to get away from the cotton fields and the oak trees.

Mamie Till-Mobley died of heart failure in Chicago two hours after our Chicago contact had spoken with her about my interview request, two days after David Thomson and I arrive to begin a modest (research) workshop, one about migration and the stage (at the Museum of Contemporary Art).

We attend her wake on the same Friday we had planned to interview her, at the Apostolic Church of God on the city's south side, near Robert's Temple Church of God where Emmett Till's cathartic, battered body was famously viewed in September 1955.

On a freezing gray Chicago morning, Mamie Till-Mobley lay like a queen, silent, with a picture of her son pinned inside her coffin.

The next day, during a break in the empty theater of the museum, I visit the upstairs' permanent collection gallery and am struck by a work of David Hammons, titled "Praying for Safety." A mixed-media work consisting of two (found?) wooden statues of Thai monks kneeling in prayer pose, perhaps twenty feet apart, with a delicate piece of thread stretched between their praying hands. A safety pin delicately balanced in the middle of the taut thread. A spiritual art pun, I thought.
Back in the theater I tell David that I want to suspend what we had been working on earlier in

the day. I don't know, I say, standing on the dimly lit stage; I'm kind of emotional today and I'd like to work on something new.

After a couple hours we come up with this physical script, memorial, and quote:
Two (black?) men with a forty-five(ish)-foot cotton string, the width of a proscenium stage. One man starts on stage, two feet out from the farthest downstage left wing; the other man is in the downstage right wing, not seen by audience. Each holds onto one end of the string, which lies loose along the length of floor.

At a given cue they simultaneously begin tying the string around their waists, pulling the string taut. Delicate bowknots that can be loosened with a quick pull from one end of the string. Their timing must be immaculate. The audience sees only one man in tying action. Once they have finished tying the string around their waists, the man onstage walks backwards, offstage, pulling the man offstage two feet onstage. With the men now reversed, they untie the string and repeat the same delicate tying structure with the string around their necks, reversing, then their penises (the pants are pulled down at this point), reversing, and then their wrists. In that order. The whole action lasts about three minutes.

Of, course the neck and penis parts are more loaded, and potentially literal, especially in how the men are tying their own nooses or how the penis is pulled erect, but by the precise timing required and everydayness of the scripted approach, and with the last image/action of the bound wrists, where one man is led more humanly, tenderly, overtly, the string and meaning evaporate.

It will take hours and hours of practice, months. The two men need to be profoundly connected in responding to one other and to the string. The timing is the dance. The rest is immaterial.

The point? Balance/imbalance. And then the few or many layers of human interaction explored: guidance, power, sex, death, race, love, partnership, and danger. (At one point in the process David tied the string around his testicles, instead of his penis, for safety reasons, he said, completely negating the point). A lot to be explored here. By fall 2004 I will have worked it so much that maybe it will no longer have an inkling of stage life. As it should be.

Date: 1/8/03 2:29 PM
From: Michelle Klein/The Walker Art Center
Just spoke with Juliet in Bruce's studio and she said that his response is a definitive "Yes." Regarding how Bruce would like to be acknowledged, Juliet said that language such as ". . . after Bruce Nauman's *Wall-Floor Positions*, 1965(?) . . ." is fine—something right along those lines.

February 2003
Second Walker Art Center workshop (with Okwui Okpolwasili, David Thomson, Djédjé Djédjé Gervais, Katherine Profeta, and James Hanaham). Where Djédjé and I re-enact Bruce Nauman's *Wall-Floor Positions*.
(The following is correspondence between Nauman's assistant and myself:)

Hello Juliet

The following are notes from the performance:

I was thinking, absurdly . . . that back in Duluth, Issac McGhie, Elmer Jackson, and Elias Clayton were surrounded by thousands of onlookers, a mob audience . . . "Oh, God, oh, God—oh God . . . I am only twenty-years-old. I have never done anything wrong. I swear I didn't. Oh, God, my God, help me."

I was surrounded by hundreds of onlookers, a gallery audience, sitting.

Moving, talking, wandering, postmodern attrition. I HAD to perform. They were so close I could feel their breath. Yikes. Nauman wouldn't have liked it, I think. I HAD to be a little spectacular, I had no choice. My partner was more like Nauman, doing a job. When I was done I was soaking wet. A dressed-up young woman said, "That looked like it hurt." The weather outdoors was eleven degrees below zero. The rock band, The Melvins, wailing away on guitars in the Walker auditorium. A retro muffled soundtrack. They weren't watching us. They were playing for another show. The wall and carpeted floor left rug burns all over my body and scalp. Didn't know till I took a bath the next day.

Thinking back, I could have sat in on The Melvins' second set when I was done, but was starving and went out instead and had a drink, after taking off my sweaty clothes and putting on dry ones.

How was it, simply? Surprisingly fun.

Later in the week I experimented with my body as Wall-Floor. A basketball hoop, a green garden hose and large piece of plywood as Wall-Floor. And two bodies and large piece of plywood as Wall-Floor. Please tell Bruce thanks a lot. This might go on forever, in fact . . .

No Room Story (twenty-five years later . . . in the future)
He turns off the light. Preparing to get lost, being lost. There he is. Where? There, behind the closed door, folded, relaxed, and then his recitation . . .

"There are no 'unexpected events of chance,' just the 'vigor, strength, control, influence' of the 'unknown' 'tricking with sleight-of-hand' its many 'expressions shown by its features' like a 'grimace' in the 'front of the head.' HA! "

Recycled, he has said this before, every time pleased with its certain continuity . . . the accident of it. Even though he does not live in this space, darkened room, featureless, he nevertheless hides in this, his private event.

It is his only chance, between now and later. He grimaces in the front of his head, his face, its expression. His tiny fingers tricking with sleight-of-hand, inside of his half-propped-up pants, between his legs. His power, control, influence, vigor. He even took off his shirt this time.

He did not expect this opportunity, aloneness, joy, now. He has language for none of what is happening, this propelled moment; it is unknown, like every other time, the seconds or hours of it. Until he knocks his head softly back against the wall where there is sound, a whispered howl and then tears, waking him momentarily, momentarily. The room stays put, has not responded, still dark, darker still, perhaps darker. If that is possible.

His head and folded body now rest against the deep pitch of the wall and floor, surfaces of nothing, that support him. Who's the hero now? He wonders, begins to think again. "No," he says, "no. There are no unexpected events of chance, ever." Eyes closed, lips reflecting little sign of recovering.

He will, has five more minutes, and then he must turn on the lights and return . . .

"Now, where is my fucking shirt?" He softly hums . . .

Hello Ralph,
It sounds excellent on so many levels, sweat and breath and rug burns; does it get any better?
I like the idea of you being spectacular and your own partner doing a job. I think both are inherent in successful creative work.
I didn't get your notes until late today; I'll share them with Bruce.

Here's to perpetual movement . . . .
Paz y luz,
Juliet

An Incomplete Chronology III

July 2002
Group workshop at Walker Art Center
with David Thomson, Djédjé Djédjé
Gervais, Katherine Profeta, Bebe Miller,
and Chelsea Lemon Fetzer.
A Lynching Site Counter-Memorial in
Duluth, Minnesota.
I first begin to think of historical water
hosings and attack dogs as theatrical de-
vices.
August 2002
Attend Otha Turner's final picnic. Sena-
tobia, Mississippi.
November 2002
Hicks Walker of Sapelo Island, Georgia,
passes. He was ninety-nine.
I meet and interview Mr. Walter Carter,
oldest man in Yazoo County, Missis-
sippi. He tells a story about a lynching
he witnessed as a boy and demonstrates
some very old juke joint dances.
January 2003
Mamie Till-Mobley passes. She was
eighty-one.
Chicago Museum of Contemporary Art
workshop.
February 2003
Second Walker Art Center workshop.
Otha Turner passes in Como, Missis-
sippi. He was 94.
November 2003
I travel to Yazoo City to meet Mr. Walter
Carter to see if he can be a part of the
performance/touring production.
Ultimately, he doesn't want to travel,
says he can't really control his bodily
functions.

A "Living Room Dance" in the former
cabin of Mississippi John Hurt, near
Avalon, Mississippi. There are no family
members present, but I do have an audience of a number of friendly "neighborhood" fans, all middle-aged white men,
with the exception of one woman, who
have Hurt's history down pat. Again I
use the song "Louis Collins," the same
song I danced to, without an audience,
on the rickety stage in Yazoo City a year
before, memorializing the lynching of
Willie Minnifield by a white mob.
When they heard that Louis was dead
All the women folk they dressed in red
Angels laid him away
Bob shot one and Louis shot two
Shot poor Collins, shot him through
and through
Angels have laid him away
I find out that the song is based on
someone Hurt actually knew, and was
most likely a black-on-black crime,
murder.
Almost final research notes: "The folks
down here continue to break my heart."
March–April 2003
Storytelling workshop at the Mark
Morris Studio with David Thomson,
James Hannaham, and Okwui Okpok-
wasili, where I hear "The Talking Drum
Story" for the first time. (The first time
Okwui remembers being called a
nigger.)

Research events #15 and #16 at the
Kitchen in New York City, where a
Dutch presenter pulls out of possibly
presenting the final production. "Sorry,
but I don't understand the atmosphere,"
he says. "I think my audience will need
a more coherent atmosphere."

May 2003

(A cultural displacement) Workshop in
Berlin at the House of World Cultures
with David Thomson, Okwui Okpokwasili, and Djédjé Djédjé Gervais, and
where I hear "Sex Story" for the first
time, Okwui's recall of the first time she
had sex with a white body.

"Now we're doing it—tongue travels to
my ass—teaching words in different
languages [broad back—marking]—
disappearing—turning into a dot—
changing . . ."

Okwui pauses . . . shakes her head, "This
is hard," she says.

I know, I know, I say, consolingly. Let's
leave it for now and come back to it another day. Why don't we take a break,
and when we come back we can practice
the second story. Does that sound OK?

Nigger Story II

In the fourth grade I had an art teacher, Ms. Hirsh, who played the djembe in the classroom to motivate us. It was the seventies in the Bronx, an era of experimentation and cultural relativism. I lived with my grandmother at the time and she had this boyfriend, William. I called him Uncle William. I remember he had a big collection of guns. He asked me if she was playing the talking drum, and I remember saying, "Well, she talks, but mostly, when we draw, she plays the drums." And he said, "No, she's playing the talking drum. She's trying to talk to you through the drum—but," he would say, "the only drum you need around here is a gun." I think she was attempting to be our muse, the kind we would respond to in the Bronx.

And I remember one day, we were making beads, it was exacting work and the drumming wasn't incredibly loud but it was a thud in my stomach and I just wanted something less bowel, more frontal lobe buzz, and I said, "I wish I could hear Bach's St. Matthew's Passion." My grandmother told me that this was the passion you felt in heaven . . . so this little girl next to me, her name was Dawn, she said, "What?" I said, "I want to hear Bach," and she said, "Yeah, whatever, nigger." And I looked at her and I said, "What, don't call me that." And she said, "Nigger." And I said, "Call me that again and I'm gonna slap you in the face." And she said, "Nigger." So I slapped her across the face, and I said, "You're the nigger."

She said, "Nigger."

And I said—slap—"You're the Nigger."

"Nigger."

Slap. "You're the Nigger."

"Nigger."

Slap. "You're the Nigger."

Now her face is beet red, her freckles make her redder, tears are streaming down her face. And Ms. Hirsh stops drumming and rushes over to us and she says, "Girls, what is going on here?" And I said, "Dawn, is calling me a nigger." She looks at Dawn and she says, "Dawn—" So Dawn interrupts: "But she was calling me a nigger." And then Ms. Hirsh looks at me and says, "Well, Okwui, Dawn can't be a nigger."

A curious ending, somewhat. I write in my notebook, "I wonder what the story would sound like with 'Baptist' instead of the word 'nigger'?" Would lose all of its rhythm for sure.

Okwui was born in the United States but is of Nigerian descent. For purposes of continuing the "nigger" conversation and research, I imagine that she is of São Tomé and Príncipe descent, and that I barely know anything about her other than she's a psychologist living in Berlin, and that she's black.

The following is a letter that I might write to her.

Dear Okwui,
I'm happy to hear that your family is safe in the mountains. I hope they are safe for a long time to come.

Safe, safety? The word has become quite amorphous in these times. The world seems so dangerous. Maybe it has always been? "Safety" seems very elusive as we move into the twenty-first century. Certainly, we know more now about the world, wherever it is we live, even São Tomé and Príncipe, and we can talk about global politics, as fucked-up as they are. This is a good thing. "Knowledge," unlike "safety," remains a powerfully coherent and relevant word.

What are your politics, simply? An impossible question? You seem such a hybrid of sorts. From an island off Africa, and then Portugal (kind of Europe), Berlin (definitely Europe!), black (?), a woman of color, a psychologist. And how many languages? A very layered psyche, no doubt. And a representation of the future of humanity, I think. Has anyone ever called you a nigger?

Are you forced, for whatever cultural reasons, to choose a simple cultural placement? I hope not. Indefinability is another good made-up word, like God.

I think an interesting problem for most "African Americans" is that we don't have enough acknowledged cultural intervention. We are a dying "ethnic" component in America. I'm not sure what that really means or if it's so important. I'm not sure if the "African American" title is a legitimate calling card; certainly it's an inept description biologically. (I'm African, French, Irish, Native American. Most black people in America are aptly polluted.) But we take what we can get, always demanding more, that's our history. And we have a clan name that keeps changing, to foster an important community/dialogue. A good start, before we disappear, inspiring other complex cultural renegades.

Anyway, it's obvious from this letter, these questions, that I know as much about black people in Europe as I do about black people in the American South—not much.

Anyway, I'm not sure when I'll be in Europe again. I'm in full production mode here, in the USA. A premiere, of a little of what you saw, in spring 2003. The director of the House of World Cultures wants to present the work in Berlin next November, 2004, but also wants to bring us back for a workshop next June. We'll see what happens.

It's August. Is all of Berlin on vacation? Are you? Such a fragrant town.

Say hello to Robin Rhode for me, if you see him.
Peace R

AIRSHIP

LONDON BRIDGE

BEAN BAG GAME

PLAYING HORSE

Process Repetition III
The Making of Come home Charley Patton

July 2003
Brooklyn Academy of Music Workshop
Okwui Okpokwasili, David Thomson, and I begin using the word "conjure" a week before the Fourth of July. At the end of the rehearsal period I say to them, OK, that's it for the counter-theater discussion, three-and-a-half years of mostly backyard research. Now it's down to a few more very structured indoor and windowless workshops and a couple more new-performer tryouts, and magically a theatrical production comes together as though none of what came before had ever happened. That's the beauty of show business.

February 2004
Pittsburgh Workshop (August Wilson Center for African American Culture)
Darrell Jones, David Thomson, Miko Doi Smith, Djédjé Djédjé Gervais, and I
Improvise
In a small room
Rage and love and nothing
A system rigorous and wild?
Using numbers
Spaces
Structure/time
Five minutes
Precisely halfway you pause
Past present future conjure
And then show Darrell
Who shows Miko, who still has a body that was being pregnant, just six weeks ago, who dances like an angel.

March 2004
Champagne-Urbana Workshop (Krannert Art Center)
Day 1. Tuesday, March 16
Snow on the ground. A final gasp of winter.
I've yet to find a title for the experience, a title about building something.

David is here. Darrell is here. And someone new, Gesel, is here. Miko is in the hospital. Okwui is acting on stage somewhere else. Djédjé is in the INS office in Connecticut. Walter Carter is in Bentonia, Mississippi, waiting out the winter.

Making art in conflict with real life.

200 dead in Spain
Five American civilians shot in a drive-by in Iraq.
They think they know who the Ohio overpass shooter is.
Kerry and Bush should just put on the gloves.
Gesel Mason. I don't know her. Saw her dance for five minutes on videotape that Darrell provided while in Pittsburgh, her only audition.

Day 2. Wednesday, March 17
Every single time I begin . . . one of these . . . I stop sleeping and cower in an insecure corner of some motel. Fuck it!
Grow the fuck up.
I think it really has something to do with my height, that I'm only five feet nine inches. (On Sapelo Island, the Sapeloans called me shorty.) And I can't grow a real beard, something like that.
Newbies: Gesel is a freedom mover by instinct. Darrel is cautious unless he's free and then he's boundless, bound to break something. I want to know why. I'll ask.

Day 3. Thursday, March 18
Work with what you have. What you don't have will not work because it isn't there.
I'm tossing my body to the wind. Everyone else follows even though maybe it's fake, like some Hollywood set-up, like the Wizard of Oz.
I've started choreographing:
Dance 1. Cool Phrase
Dance 2. Onion Duet
Djédjé has arrived. Miko is out of the hospital but thinks she may not be able to return.
I know a little of what I'm doing. A shift.
Thank god for OutKast, Sister Gertrude, and Leftovercrack!

The surviving cast:
Djédjé
Darrell
David
Okwui
Gesel
We begin by making a dance called Mississippi by using these names and keywords:
Willie Minnifield—no audience, front and back, exposed.
Emmett Till—whistle, describing a penis (a "dick"), drowning. Not forgetting. (I'm not sure why I decide to leave out "Bye-baby," but I do.)
Medgar Evers—open car door, shot, crawl, frozen in time.

OK, everyone moves like they move. Allow them all the freedom that Gesel is confiscating. Boldly.
Demanding that they are different. Protest beauty!

These are my beginning, ongoing questions, I announce:
1. Where does one find transformation in our separate modern dance experiences?
2. How does one use, how can one use, how should one use a volatile historical fact as creative fodder? Where is the freedom and obligation in the process and result?
3. How does one translate my particular private research experiences and or my referential/conjured dancing statements, in a given rehearsal situation?
And as soon as these questions leave my mouth, the privacy of my head, I'm a little embarrassed and try to disfigure my earnestness. Talking, I say, showing a little frustration is some elaborate transmission of the nervous system being creative, organically making personal ge-

netic (neural) sense (most times, if we're lucky) within layer upon layer of any given body/emotion life exchange . . . "I see a bird, a blue bird, in a tree . . . is it a pecan tree?" A conversion, a stand-in for something else more purely chemical, something more stimulated, because that's how it functions: like art, like theater. Talking tries to name it. And at this point in our pre-nano/post-enlightenment humanness we can call everything something.

So, will it be useful talking about any of this stuff or might we leave it to the more mute thought process of the body? I ask.

The group answers with a very tricky question, "What's a buck dance?"

I have to go back to an audiotaped interview made in 1991, with the Philadelphia hoofer, Lavaughn Robinson. (Transcribed by Katherine Profeta, my dramaturge.)

Ralph: So what is a buck dance?

Lavaughn: See, everyone does their own interpretation . . . One thing a tap dancer does not like to be called is a natural buck dancer. See, buck dancing came off the plantation, see what I'm saying?

[Lavaughn goes on to explain that hoofers are tap dancers, who came off of the street. Buck dance came off of the plantation. Hoofing is another name for tap.]

Lavaughn: Buck is like the hoedown.

Ralph: Was it for them, or was it for the master?

Lavaughn: No, they were doing it for their own pleasure, and the ones that were good were doing it for the slave masters, you dig where I'm coming from? They have guys today that make their living doing buck dance.

Ralph: Literally today?

Lavaughn: Yeah, because I worked with a couple of them . . . played guitar, sang blues, and buck danced. But see, here's the difference. Buck dancing don't have no story to it. There's no story. If you knew anything about hoofing you know . . . We look at buck dancing as if to say, oh man . . . [inflection as if fed up with it]. You dig where I'm coming from?

Ralph: Now, going back to buck dancing, since there's no story—what . . . so, are we talking about a rhythmic difference, or a . . .

Lavaughn: No, we're talking about the rhythmic difference, because the rhythm is there but it ain't, you understand what I'm trying to say? It's not like [demonstrates buck rhythm, then a tap rhythm. After the second, says:] You see the story there? You see when you buck dance you don't have no pattern.
Ralph: You're improvising.

Lavaughn: Right! You take a buck dancer that's featuring buck dancing. If you tell him to do what he just did again, he might not be able to do that. Not like he did it the first time. You got a lot of life that comes from out of that. That's another thing too, man, because I've worked with buck dancers . . .

Enough, I think, and turn off the tape recorder.

And then, facing the group again, I continue . . .
Brothers and sisters, I had thought it might be fun to try to create the great black American epic never written (Toni Morrison's *Beloved* and Ed Jones's *The Known World*, and also I suppose, *Narrative of the Life of Frederick Douglass*, Dubois's *The Souls of Black Folk*, Hurston's *Their Eyes Were Watching God*, Toomer's *Cane*, Wright's *Native Son*, Ellison's *Invisible Man*, Butler's *Kindred* . . . Styron's *The Confessions of Nat Turner*, and almost everything that Faulkner wrote, all these aside). The prosaic and the myth. And this question: When is a culture allowed to be mythologized? Has the 400-year black experience in America earned that right? Of course there is a modern reality that makes some of this question complicated, almost irrelevant.

"Which one of us gets hosed? That's what I want to know," David says. "I think it's gotta be you, Ralph, as part of your baptismal passage. Heh, heh, wading in the freezing water at the beginning . . . traversing time later on."

Fuck you, David, I say.

Day 4. Friday, March 19
Today I will talk about the earth.
Wind
Horse
Water
Psychology
And memory
Segregated memory
Reconstructed memory
Instinctively trying to match past/current events with one's past experiences/history. There's no permanent record there. Placing an interpretation on what you see/remember. Conflicting accounts can be useful proving that something did happen.

I work with the others, waiting for Miko to call, as she becomes another ghost in the process like Angelo and Bebe and James. Where are the traces? How does one choreograph spirit? What's another word?
James, James Hanaham, created a major shift in my performance thinking, his counter-dance presence, a different kind of thinking and physicality, movement as a series of peculiar short sentences written with the body. Although I eventually lost most of that wonderment (James went to graduate school to write a novel), and I ultimately returned to an art physicality I'm more familiar with.
I'm choreographing something every day, so far, on modern dancers, except for Djédjé. Why not? Trying to bend it off of a modern dance stage.

Forced to wonder/wander boundaries.

Not as simple as on or off or enter and exit.

Then what is it?

This first dance is for Miko, because she's not here and unlike the other absentees is supposed to be here. A quandary. This part is clear.

Dance 1. She's Not There

Dance 2. We put Mississippi and Duluth together and call it Mississippi/Duluth

Dance 3. (Peeling an) Onion. (Parts 1,2,3)

Day 5. Saturday, March 20

Poor Darrel finally broke something, sprained his ankle, but the photo session was fun, too much fun, one might say, for Darrell especially. "Wilding," that's what the process feels like so far.

Words for the day:

Limp

Sit

Bring on the Africans

I have no idea what these last four words mean.

It is the one-year anniversary of the Iraq war and I am not marching.

Not exactly.

Re: Remembering Birmingham II. Krannert Workshop
So what's happening with the hose? I'd really hate to forfeit this element, especially given that the attack-dog inclusion became a little too complicated.
Best
R

Re: Re: Remembering Birmingham II. Krannert Workshop
Well, the Fire Training Institute is willing to give us a demonstration of the hose system. They will not agree to fire it at a person, but will set up a demonstration with a mannequin. They will not do this if the weather is freezing outside.
I propose that you all give me some general availability for the next three weeks. We go out to the training institute and videotape a demonstration.
Randy: It sounds like they will be able to educate you on nozzle sizes/fittings.
Bruce: Please forward to anyone else who should be present.
Best
Stephen

Day 6. Sunday, March 21
Imagining an architecture. Building something to last a few months at most.
I've been making the same work for almost ten years and this particular part for almost four years. In that time I have been more and more absorbed by the practice, my interpretation of a practice of "research." This research has been pivotal to my thinking and art action. (Perhaps "inaction" is a better way to describe it.) I've not done a lot of performing in this process. I have spent a lot of time, watching, listening, agreeing, disagreeing, feeling arrogant and stupid.
The stage has become an active stranger, a dutiful adversary, in how it possibly represents something more than it presents. It is a demanding space, the stage space, but not an impossible predicament. The stage is only a stage, nothing more, however mysterious. Its expectations, societal, private . . . are the source of some confusion, some radical brilliance, and not a little of the mundane. Tell a story, any story.
Being on the Colwell Playhouse stage, white cyc, grey Marley floor extended (which will be white later), the depth of field, perspective, upstage/downstage, has been a complete surprise even though this was the plan. I'm composing as though these five bodies are miles away from one another. Isolation, and the illusion of intimacy. Everybody looks pretty faintly elegant, dignified already.
The stage-right memory space is still a big wonder. The rows of high school auditorium chairs look great! What to do with them? No attic space yet, but we'll play with the robot camera and some aluminum stage ladders on Tuesday. Lot's of good problems with this act for sure.

Sixteen new keywords to generate movement:
Wind
Ground (Hallow?)
Memorial (Counter)
Water
Horse (Animal)

Fury
Flurry
Praise
Rapture (?)
Spiral
Circle
Spiral
Surrender
Courage
Trust
Shaky elegance

There is a certain amount of suffering that goes on in the world, dignified.

Later
Day 7. Monday, March 22
It is always about courage. There is very little else. Unless we sleep. And Death is no escape.

Day 8. Tuesday, March 23
To Rick Murray: Do you see the space between them? Do we keep the room wide open (visible) so we see the space between bodies?

"Yes and we also just see the loneliness, a single small place. Always drastic and soft until we see the light box, and even that is only a smaller version of the same place, squared."

Suddenly feeling claustrophobic.
But why?
Convince me that the hosing space and the attic space are absolutely necessary, not from an emotional context but from a light-shift change-of-view, even if you have doubts.
Who?
Prove it, so that I can sleep.
What?
At this point I stop talking about Bruce Nauman.

Key events later in the day:
Falling and trying again and again.
Lots of body circles moving through space.
An opera about a lynching or two.
A sense of humor will save this thing yet.

Day 9. Wednesday, March 24
Mars Rover believed on beach of ancient sea!
Memorial: Rather to be implicit or explicit?
Your body and the story: that's the science.
A note for me: Be patient and tell those that need to be told what it is they are doing well and improperly. I am alone in this.

Day 14. Monday, March 29
"Loneliness is not an important form of suffering. It's undeniable, but it's just not significant."
—Anne Carson

Day 20. Sunday, April 4
The fall tour has a giant hole . . . two cancellations, for a work yet to be made.
What's inside the giant hole? Water? Dirt? Black . . . nothing?
What else can happen? All else will happen, will happen for a performance that has yet to be made.

I dance my opinion clearer than I think it.
Where does the oblique become famous? On stage. And how famous and/or empty? That will remain a mystery.
It is only a physically academic exercise in theater, after all. That is all it can be, we are not marching, rioting, being spat on, being lynched, not really. And we are angry about other things.
Nevertheless, every time we are on stage we become fire.
We are still being called nigger, call ourselves that. A brief utopia.
Our bodies and their science, that's the story, each of us.
In this way we are like the early protesters, shaky elegance, with no idea what's going to happen. We just know we need to be here.

Day 21. Monday, April 5
I worked so hard yesterday that I was able to read a book before I slept, Gaddis, *Agape Agape*, a few pages.

Day 27. Sunday, April 11
Easter. I cannot write. Too hurried. Filling gaps, at least in my thinking about things. One more dance to make with real bodies, not choreographic images, I imagine.
The problem for this afternoon (the whole world): I'm trying to do too much, to say too much, dancing too much. There is so much to say.
Unsettled. I've mostly lived in motels for nine years, with one more year to go. The art practice? It's a giant project . . . way too big. But I meditate and think, yes, think, nearly five hours a day. The rest of the time I'm telling people what to do, how they can help. It's been interesting. And I've been choreographing! Haven't done that for four years.
Parts of this piece will be on the mark and parts will miss . . . time seems to be the adversary. Like always. And there are just too many people around. I do have lots of support. OK, got to spend a few hours thinking . . . or else my crew will run all over me, or away.

Tonight I'll read another book, a little Gilles Deleuze this time, and if I'm lucky it too will be useless and I can fall asleep.

Day 28. Monday, April 12
"I love Morrissey, too bad he's gay." Gloombabear writes in the uploader comments on YouTube, for The Smiths, "Please, Please, Please, Let Me Get What I Want."

Another, DanFret123, writes, "How much does this song make you want to throw an England flag into the sea?"

While inspecting a large pile of speaker cable, Lulu Indelicato tells me that Morrissey and the Smith's were his teenage blues. "I even wore my hair like Morrissey for a while . . . and stopped dating." After about an hour Leadbelly comes humming through the sound system, a test, another three-minute magnum opus about the predicament of wakefulness:

Black girl black girl
don't you lie to me
tell me where did you sleep last night.

To Rick Murray: Will this transfiguration I'm attempting be seen as a conversion or a revolution?
"How bout . . . transformation as time viewed on an empty stage slowly gathering history as the performance progresses." Rick says, exhausted and inspired. He has been in the theater since he got off the plane. A little odd, feels like we're opening the work in the next couple days; we're not, everything will be different, more developed by the fall, the lights as well. In the meantime we find precision in the hours of a single day, where there is always some compromise.

"In the house setting up, I saw Djédjé dancing, spinning in circles in a circle for about fifteen minutes in work-light. And I thought it was the best thing ever, I couldn't believe it. Then when I saw the real rehearsal—the group rehearsal—it was only about three minutes. And I missed the other twelve minutes."
Video designer Mike Taylor and I had a good talk over the weekend on the phone. She was here and then had to leave, but will be back soon, and really needs to be here now for us to get any reasonable video interface; my friends from the South, an authentically mediated background to whatever else it is the rest of us come up with. Making the rest of us look and sound like intriguing human art material. Or amusing—that would be OK too.

Christian Marclay has some new music on the way to go along with the cut-up LP scratch rhythms and excerpted grunts, trains, and church bells . . . that we already have, making Otha Turner and John Cage either proud or roll over in their parallel graves.
In the meantime, I ask Katherine Profeta to try to find some six degrees of separation between Marclay, Janis Joplin, Jacques Brel, Roland Hayes, and the Lochamer Liederbuch.

Waiting for an update from the Face2Face animators for the Baldwin cartoon and for permission from the Baldwin estate to use his dangerously excerpted words.
And the wooden horse table, my Red Pony.
How's it coming along?
"It's a pretty rickety, almost falling down kind of walk. I like it a lot. It seems like the kind of walk that something that's not supposed to be able to walk would do . . . and it can fall down too!" Doug.

The cast continues to badger me about the wooden horse table. "Why, what for?" they ask. I tell them it's probably the most important moving body in the show (on four legs) and most likely no one will see it.

Day 30. Wednesday, April 14
The hose works. Now what to do with it?
I felt like I had been swimming, while standing, a fire-station test dummy . . . ears and eyes showered by too much water.
Step 2. We dance in light.

Day 34. Sunday, April 18
I have a plan. An elusive narrative.
Most days, so far, I am confident.
We need to practice the hose . . . brutal joy.
Last night I watched videos of Jimi Hendrix and Janis Joplin and had to have a cigarette. And then I started to tear and write . . .

Wind—If you are really quiet you can distinguish its rhythm.
Ground (Hallow)—Every inch of the white and black floor.
Memorial (Counter)—At least an hour of this work is that, probably more.
Water—Waiting intervention, when you stop thinking, ever present.
Horse (Animal)—Never loses its dignity. That's why they shoot them when they go lame.
Fury—Whisper wildly.
Praise—Share the joy when you remember that it is possible.
Rapture—If you find it, keep the explanation to yourself.
Spiral—She's Not There 1(Beautiful), for a few seconds.
Circle—Djédjé Djédjé cleans the space.
Spiral—She's Not There 2 (Brutally in love).
Surrender—Eyes open.
Courage—Offstage. Onstage, you have no choice.
Trust—Walking.
Shaky Elegance—What happens in front of the plywood boards.

If you need to say something, suddenly, say "whew," quietly.

Day 37. Wednesday, April 21
I hit another wall. Tear my right meniscus in the hosing pool. The obvious danger of calling on these ghosts. And then the anxiety of finishing for now reappears, again. Keep it simple. And whatever happened to improvisation? Oh yeah, forgot about that. Music is a problem; it's not (deadly) alive enough. Music as historical, present-day reference, clues to memory, placement, and recall. I wish Otha Turner was having another picnic, I'd just invite everyone to that and be done with it.

I need a little help, so I call Katherine Profeta, whose job it is to ask me questions about what it is I think I'm thinking and what it is I think I'm not. I recite this quote from Deleuze. I wasn't lucky after all, the reading wasn't useless.

"Fantasy forges fictive casual claims, illegitimate rules, simulacra of belief, either by conflating the accidental and the essential or by using the properties of language (going beyond experience) to substitute for the repetition of similar cases actually observed, a simple verbal repetition that only simulates its effect. It is thus that the liar believes in his lies by dint of repeating them . . . we are not threatened by error, rather and much worse, we bathe in delirium."

"Ai yi yi," she says and tells me she'll get on a plane the next day.

Day 38. Thursday, April 22
OK, Okwui, in the beginning I'd like you to walk onstage like Janis Joplin, an extremely sensitive and talented ugly white girl from Port Arthur, Texas, who "didn't hate niggers," who early on was completely in love with Bessie Smith and Leadbelly . . .
And the rest of us will go from there.

The lights go down . . .

Research event #23. A run-thru with some of what we've come up with thus far.
The parts flow even as the whole halts. Darrell's ankle is better and he is boundless again.
Katherine likes what was. The smaller, more intimate event versions, with more me being more intimate and honest (unreliably). And now it's a lot about the giant space of the theater. One person, one idea will not fit, would disappear. Like in the world, I say. And Katherine readies her defense.

"What's the spine?" she asks, as I start to nod (I am so tired) and then David Thomson, standing nearby, my dependable doppelganger says, "I start thinking about how everyone's main action in the piece, and throughout the epic, is to journey toward what might be home . . . with all the different theories of what home is to sift through, and all the inevitable detours along the way . . . but a desire for that running like a current throughout."

I'm wide-awake now. A spine?

Well, there's the landscape.
The landscape here has much to do with the temporal. A shifting cultural belief system. The space divided into these spaces:

1. The memory space. Empty theater (high school auditorium) seats. Nothing happens there, no one uses it, or its use is questionable, it's just there, sort of, like memory.

2. An attic space. For transcendence, transcendence as finding "lost play." Djédjé and Darrell engage in a suspended wrestling match. Djédjé eventually retrieves a basketball hoop and recites the James Hanaham solo, a trace. Djédjé and Darrell are also the lover in Okwui's sex story.

3. Absent space. The primary stage. An extended open space (into the audience) for "modern dance?" "Modern dance theater?" The ultimate etherealness of these enactments?

4. The secondary spaces. The spaces between.

5. The pool space. Water . . . shower . . . baptismal . . . Kelly Ingram Park in Birmingham . . . another Boneyard . . . nature and how nature is historic and violent and playful and cleansing, I think.

6. The documentary space/roving video screen. The real world, mediated, out of context and portable. A clandestine attempt at truth to ground this thing.

7. Baldwin screen. An out-of-context animated Buddha . . . a narrator, in the audience space. Familiar and yet koanic?

8. The plywood walls. Moments of placement, raw, basic. A temporary Wall-Floor Position.

9. Music. Sonic memory. A series of referential contexts externalized. Creating multiple contexts beyond the more private/personal/coded process investigations. More for the audience than me.

10. Of course there are Rick's illuminations.

11. The audience . . .

12. A title?

Placehouse

HomeHorse

HouseHorse

Houseland

No Room

No Wall

Water Wall

How can you stay in the house all day and not go anywhere?

House Silence

Silent House

House Silent

Quiet House

Every House

Come home Charlie Patton

How to make a good house not half-bad

The title becomes a problem, a real pain in the ass. How do you signify a place whose place is purposefully dislocated, a planted lie, shifting, like the fault-line plates in the earth?

A shaky spine.
And its flexuous vertebrae. Starting from the bottom.
Arne Bontemps's "A Summer Tragedy" revisited and interpreted might be the sacrum, the base, what we're dancing from. Not really part of the great black American epic (never-written) canon, because it's such a perfect short story. But there are a couple things in the story that I find easiest to connect with everything else that is happening in the stage work.
1. The love story of Jeff and Jennie. Jeff and Jennie are grand and caring partners to the end. "The tortured and noble and suffering and loving," illuminating everything else around them.
2. It is also a story of magnificent passage, like Okwui's coming-of-age, nigger, and sex stories . . . and Elias's mediated story (Me, in Duluth. Elias is also all of us, of course.)

Us. The performers are the vertebrae, the matter and articulation of the remaining upper regions of this work's spine. Unless this flexuous pillar happens to be falling. Which it quite often is. I can argue most of the performers' probing work as fitting into these not-so-simple human experiences:
1. The long dance section we're working on can certainly be read as a story of partnership.
2. Djédjé's solos, his noble spinning, aloneness, diligence, and curious alienation is an extension of his ongoing passage to America and his journey through the Geography trilogy.
3. The communal dances (Mississippi/Duluth, Rapture, Orbs, etc.): again, spinning, aloneness, diligence, and alienation, shared. Love, nobility, a community, remembering, conjuring, reverently. And then all of it, these lovely boundaries, dissolving (briefly) in the new unattainable Ecstasy improvisation. A three-minute Dionysian romp, unfinished.
4. My own placement, as I have to be here, is an important passage for me in the micro and macro of this new work and in the culmination of this ten-year trilogy. Important, because at any moment I feel as though I could disappear.

What's that? I say. Katherine had said something, something about home, or maybe that I was limping. I missed it.
"Yes!" David shouts, and then says, "Leaving it on an unfinished yet resolved note. Over the cliff . . ."
Katherine is taking notes. And I assume whatever she said wasn't that important.
Down the dirt road blues, I say anyway.

I'm going away to a world unknown.
I'm going away to a world unknown.
I'm worried now, but I won't be worried long . . .

MI INTERESSA l'ARCHITETTURA

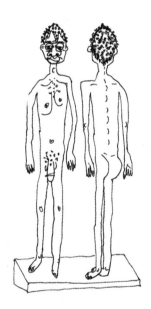

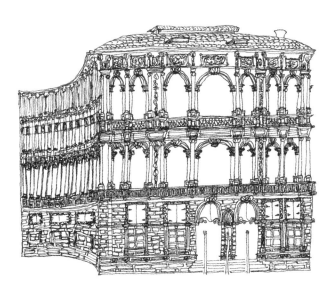

July 2004

Feeling little to no apprehension about any new impending mysteries and to get away from all this chatter, I leave town, without a premonition that something revealing might happen. I don't even notice the weather.

All by myself, limping, I return to Europe, a master landscape of the art lie, an incorrigible illusion, along with some brilliant, requisite truth. But not Berlin this time (Berlin, where you can see Beuys you can't see anywhere else). This time, Italy. Lake Como, a Bellagio residency, where I sit, mostly behind a simple wooden desk looking out a tiny window, overlooking a perfect lake, thinking mostly about Mississippi, and finish writing a rough draft of the script and land a title.

Come home Charley Patton
(Whose life story isn't reliable, who sang about "going away to a world unknown," who had his throat cut and was married eight times, whose music I never danced to, in my living room or anyone else's; I never even tried.)

A stranger. And I will keep it that way.

I bring the title and the rough draft of the script with me on a side trip to Venice, crowded, gorgeous Venice. Too crowded, so I step inside an upscale African art shop (to look at the remains of an incomprehensible Africa), where after a short time the Italian proprietor asks, "What's that?" points, grabs my crotch for a few seconds, and then apologizes. "Mi dispiace . . . I'm sorry," he says. "I thought it would be OK. I didn't really believe you came here to buy— anything."

"Che cos'é?" Fuck you, that's what that is. And by the way, can you smell my heart, asshole? I say.

I need a year in the mountains, any mountains, where's there's no fucking culture, growing a beard and shit, swearin' and smoking all day long, I think to myself, as I limp out the shop's front door.

August 2004

I bring the title and the rough draft of the script back to America. To New York City, on a bad knee, which has gotten worse, rehearsing with the performers at Brooklyn Academy of Music, taking lots of taxis, discover Celebrex before it's banned, and soon return to the Krannert and continue to refine the movement and words we've been negotiating for months and years.

My knee gets better over time. It had to, having no choice, and the rough draft script becomes less rough.

In the meantime, a close and remarkable friend, Homer Avila, dies of chondrosarcoma, in New York City. A rare cancer. Yes, how perfect that an artist should die of something rare. On the one leg and hip he had left, after the earlier surgery, he had crutched his way to a dance concert the night before, applauded at the end, checked himself into Sloan-Kettering, called some friends, said goodbye, and died. He sent me an email a few weeks before, while I was a week or two away from a dress rehearsal, saying, "Hi Ralph. Life is bold and hardly even. Love H."

I call Miko right away. Miko, who was supposed to be part of this but couldn't, she just couldn't. Are you all right, I say.

"Yes, I'm fine. Please don't worry. Everything will be fine. I survived," she says.

September 2004 (the last memorial for now)
Yes, hardly even and bold, I say to Homer's ghost while listening to Nina Simone's version of "Here Comes the Sun." Another ghost, one of many I'm dancing with. My body is managing. I have two costumes, because one will get wet every night because I'm the one that should get hosed, I say. We are all managing. Gesel has grown an Afro. Darrell is transformed, something to do with being broken up a few months back. Djédjé is always perfect. This was not always the case. Okwui has learned all her lines and songs, as she becomes Janis Joplin as Nina Simone, and also Jenny from "A Summer Tragedy," and me and the horse . . . David gets better and better and blacker and blacker.

There are so many people involved in this endeavor and I am grateful. I share my Celebrex with everyone.

Homer, like most of the others, won't necessarily know what I'm talking about, but he'll surely know what it is I'm doing.

BAER BALDWIN WITH THE NECK OF A BOXER (FRASIERESQUE)

NINA SIMONE MISSING A FACE

SHE STRONGLY FEELS THAT TRUTH IS THE REAL YARDSTICK FOR
HUMANITY'S SURVIVAL. AND SHE LOVES HER FELLOW MAN.

Opening Story
September 21, 2004

Describe it. Whatever it is, describe it. If you can describe it, you may be able to control it. You may be able to answer the tyranny of what seems to be external. —James Baldwin

And then Katherine who's been reading Baldwin, says, "He also said this: in order to write about a place you have to be able to 'sit down and turn your back to it.'"

Yes, James Baldwin, yes, I say.

"And he said this . . . 'I think all artists are religious.'"

Oh my Jesus! I say. (Borrowing a line from some person and or situation in almost every single trip I had ever taken down South.)

And then I quote Shakespeare, I can't help myself (although many years later Katherine informs me it's not Shakespeare, not at all, it's Wordsworth):

". . . When the light of sense goes out, but with a flash that has revealed the invisible world."

The lights go down . . .

I imagine walking onstage, into a spotlight, holding a trumpet, my grandfather's trumpet, which I've borrowed from my uncle Trent, without getting shot. And Mattie was wrong; it was in his attic. (And Trent was once a boy full of innocence, would take a BB gun and shoot robins and sparrows out of the trees, the fat ones, would make a fire out in the field and feather, skin, and roast the little fat birds on sticks, eating the breasts.)

I begin by saying this: To dance about a place you have to . . .

And then I turn my back to the audience, ask a stagehand for a microphone and stand, and now amplified, continue (with little sense of humor).

Will it be useful talking about what's about to happen, or might we leave it to the wordless thought process of the body, my body? I ask.

I suppose we could talk about the theater of what's about to happen more easily than the rest. Because at this moment, right here, now, what else is there? I'm here on stage and you're out there, formally waiting for something to happen, a story. So let's start with theater, that kind of body.

I began with dance as biological physical theater, the theater of my body forming language. I now reside in my dance as a terrifically broad question of existence or a series of questions of existence. These impossible questions become my practice. (The sound of this last sentence comes off very pat.)

And then Katherine . . . Katherine as Mattie, as Mamie Till-Mobley, as Memphis Minnie, as Mrs. Helen Kent, as Frank Stokes, as Mississippi Fred Mcdowell, as one-hundred-year-old Walter Carter, as Bruce Nauman, as James Baldwin . . . planted, stands and calls out from the audience, "Questions? What are these impossible questions? Maybe you can't answer them, but do you have to obscure them? What would happen if you stopped right there where you are, turned around to face us, started over and articulated them in detail? Would that be so bad?"

That would be awful, I think to myself, pretending to be a little shocked that Katherine has interrupted me. No, I say, I won't stop, I can't stop, and I won't turn around; it is my passion. (And now I begin to raise my voice.) And in defense of my passions, I obscure. I obscure because my real life is spirited, yes, but also sloppy and mundane. I obscure from you most of what I eat, sleep, and shit . . . I share and show only what I find possible to construct, think, imagine, (mask?) outside of the prosaic dailiness of my existence. I share and show a bunch of deliberately different questions to the audiences outside of my own private thinking and questioning. These public questions, questions developed because of an audience, are questions I can direct, and articulate, fictively. I do my job, my work, and by working obscure my human fragility, showing only the fiction of my fears, if I so choose.

So maybe before there are questions, any questions, there is only discursive thinking. Life, unpackaged, unpresentable. Voiceless. And by obscuring I'm allowed to have a voice . . .

The audience applauds.

Now, may I continue? I say, quite moved by this response.

"Yes, please, go on; I'd like to hear the rest," Katherine, she, he, they say.

I begin with the body, no way around it. The body as place, memory, culture, and as a vehicle for a cultural language.

And so of course I'm in a current state of the wonderment of the politics of form. That I can feel both emotional outrageousness with my body as a memory map, an emotional geography of a particular American identity, and that I can reflect on empirical design. How mining a charged history can be in contradiction to a formalist art process and the separation that has to happen, transforming a culturally inherited abstract rage into art (play), a sharing. Changing the fundamental natures of race, art, and rage as I understand them.

My present American conflict becomes more internalized. Ludwig Wittgenstein, from a family of Christians, who considered himself a Jew, "my people," he called them, who no doubt had little practical use for jargon—words like race, culture, and rage—offered that there is no equivalent between what seems to be the case and what is the case. Only the tension prevails. What shape to give this tension interests me a great deal. An interest beyond race, cultural politics (art?), and maybe even rage, which seems very much aligned with love, in how they both have aspects of the divine. Although love is supposed to transcend empathic curiosity. Is supposed to.

What am I trying to say?

(At this point there is music, over the sound system, a theme song from the epic western movie *How the West Was Won*, romantic American landscape music, soothing . . .)

OK, so let's say that art, as most of us like to consider it, is beyond the mire of a soul's unfiltered messiness. But art, as I appreciate it, is also not confined to transformation; it does not triumph over all. Sometimes, at its best, it sits in shit, nonfiction. And poor. Also possibly fake.

But then what is it?

Meaning is always constituted. Basically, whatever it is it should have a beginning and an ending that allow an audience, a witness like you, to come and to go, to walk away appreciating or not appreciating an experience clearly not your own, which is why you can love it or hate it or feel nothing at all.

Otherwise it's desk art, faultlessly private, or a luminous and barely seen "Living Room Dance," absolute and incontrovertible acts. Sub Rosa. Or audaciously bold and inversely defined:

After the September 11 attacks I told a friend I thought those jumping from the buildings were like dancers. She was outraged and I explained. Dancers, I said, that's how I identify with them. Bodies, unbounded, in space, giant space, and the unknown. For me, letting my body fall onto a stage has always been a brutal consideration . . . until now. And then I pause. And turn around facing them. Am speechless. *How the West Was Won* fades, to silence.

Silence. And more silence . . .

Beautiful and interminable.

I so wish I could blow this trumpet, I think to myself.

A child (maybe eight) clutching a program and reeking of gravitas came up to me in the audience before curtain, watched me mess with the computer, and said, "What's this about?" I said, "it's kind of about being black in the South, in America, now and not so long ago, but it's also kind of about being anyone anywhere anytime." The kid said OK, and went back to his seat. —Mike Taylor

Come home Charley Patton

Pre-show Horse film fades to Stomp girl/drummer film

Baldwin appears, to watch film/audience, 45 sec into Stomp girl

(1:10 from top of Stomp) RL enters

(1:30 from top of Stomp) Baldwin text 1

Um, I recognize this landscape. The interior and exterior landscape. The tortured and noble and suffering and loving . . . It illuminates the people all around me.

Ralph text in response to Baldwin/w/Nauman board

Ralph: Yeah—me, too. I was there. Port au Prince, 1995.

David: Liar.

Ralph: OK, how about Sapelo Island, Georgia. I was there.

David: Maybe.

Ralph: OK, OK, Duluth, definitely Duluth. Yeah, the tortured and noble, the tragic love story. It all begins with me in the water, there.

Stomp girl/drummer film ends

Boneyard film begins as Baldwin fades and Djédjé enters attic.

I'd like to read to you from my favorite short story . . .

Once a year, or maybe twice . . .

There was a wedding . . . among his kinfolk.

Ralph: There was no wedding. I read wrong; that part of the story refers to sprucing up, for some special occasion. How one takes something off and puts something else on when they're about to go out into the world to discover something amazing. That's right, right? . . . Hey [whistle]

David (in memory space): Huh, what's that?

Ralph: There was no wedding?

David: I think so; no, I'll make sure to ask later . . .

Boneyard (1:13 later/from end of first Boneyard text)
"Jennie, Jennie," he called. "What's that Jeff?" His wife's shrunken voice came out of the adjoining room like an echo. It was hardly bigger than a whisper.

David: What did she say?

Ralph: I don't know—she was whispering. But I understood Jeff's question. He asked, "Baby, the ladder to the attic, is that where we is goin'?"

David: How sweet.

Boneyard (1:41 from end of 2nd Boneyard text)
"You oughta could do a heap mo' wid a thing like that'n me—beingst as you got yo' good sight."

"Looks like I oughta could," he admitted. "But ma fingers is gone democrat on me. I get all mixed up in the looking-glass and can't tell witcha way to twist the devilish thing."

Jennie sat on the side of the bed and old Jeff got down on one knee while she tied the bowknot. It was a slow and painful ordeal for each of them in this position. Jeff's bones cracked, his knee ached, and it was only after half-a-dozen attempts that Jennie worked a semblance of a bow into the tie . . .

(40 sec later) Close your eyes.

End of Boneyard film. Mama B film.

Ralph: Jennie's eyes were closed; her lips reflected little sign of why she and Jeff were getting all dressed up. She stood up from the bed and walked over to the old rickety chair nearest the closet. As she sat down to unwrap her dress, the old chair finally broke underneath her. "'Bout time," she laughed and started singing, small verses of three or four songs the world had completely forgotten, or never knew. By the end of the day, she and Jeff would drive off a cliff together. [Baldwin reappears]

Jennie, Jeff, and those they left behind . . . the boy, Aunt Tempy, and Uncle William with his everyday gun collection and icebox full of frozen turkeys . . . So, Mr. Baldwin, there's that story, there's the other stories, there's the long dance in the middle, the one with the questionable soul music, that has very little to do with the stories. There's all this.
Where is the center . . . or some focal point? [improv. until Baldwin speaks]

Baldwin text 2
Make it happen on the boy's birthday! Make everything happen on John's birthday and make everything be seen through him.

Ralph: John, huh? . . . John? . . . Isn't there a better name?

David: How 'bout Elias?

Ralph: Yeah, Elias. And what was that you said? "If he moves here, he'll—I mean I'll—jump there, and then if I move here—I mean me! And I do this, he'll go—I'll—jump? Uh, to do that. And when I make my next move, he'll—then I got him. Or something. And it always worked. Sorta."

Baldwin thinks about it. Gesel . . . Okwui enters for Intro
Baldwin fades.

Intro/MS/Rapture/Duluth/Pre-ecstasy

Okwui
(chair fall)

Hi, I'm Ralph Lemon.

(recording starts, Okwui lip-syncs to it) This song was recorded years ago by the great Nina Simone. I always wanted to do it, so I did it, and I'm gonna do it again, right now:

(song: "Little Girl Blue," lip-synced)

That was Ralph doing Janis doing Nina doing Rogers and Hart from the musical *Big Top*. Now this is me doing Nina doing Jacques Brel doing Jacques Brel:

(song: "Ne me quitte pas," lip-synced then live)

Jennie would have loved that song. But this next song I want to share with you was one of her absolute favorites. It's a Roland Hayes song.
He sang spirituals but he also sang German love songs, and those were the ones she liked best. This one she would sing as a lullaby to her grandson when he would visit summers.
"OK, Elias. Close your eyes."

Okwui/Roland Hayes song lyrics/my joy would be more smiling/in English/ to Marclay composition
My joy would be overflowing,
would good fortune come to my aid;
Should good fortune turn toward me,
it would soothe my yearning pain . . .

I am the light dance

RL solo

Okwui/my joy would be more smiling #2/in German

Duluth #2/Freedom (*How the West Was Won* music)

Baldwin text 3 (audio only, over music?)
I thought to myself, if I do this he'll jump there. If he jumps there and I do this, he'll go there. And if I make my next move, if he jumps here, then I got him. And it always worked.

Nigger Story (outline form)

—Mrs. Taylor (fourth grade)
        –played the djembe in art class
        –played in recess when we'd play horseshoes or basketball
        –wanted to be our muse?

—She would say: "Respect the experience. The question of who has ownership of history, memory, spirit is unanswerable, so just respect the experience; that's as good as it gets."

        –remember we were in fourth grade—huh?

—Living with my Aunt Tempy and Uncle William
        –Uncle William: talking drum?
        –me: talks, and drums, but not both
        –William: the only kind of drum you really need around here is a gun.
        –w/William everything always came back to guns -> shotgun collection

—My birthday
        –bead-making, Mrs. T playing djembe; exacting work, different colored beads
        –wanted to hear something less X more Y -> Verdi's *Otello*
            (X=heavy, stomach, gut Y=light, ethereal, sweet)
        –it was my birthday, should hear what I want
        –girl Lily overhears: "What?"
        –music in heaven; finding God in heaven

I said, "I want to hear Verdi," and she said, "Yeah, whatever nigger."

And I looked at her and I said, "What did you call me?"

And she said, "Nigger."

And I said, "Call me that again and I'm gonna slap you in the face."

And she said, "Nigger."

So I slapped her across the face. I said, "You're the Nigger."

She said, "Nigger."

And I said—slap—"You're the Nigger."

"Nigger"

Slap. "You're the Nigger."

"Nigger"

Slap. "You're the Nigger."

[return to outline form]

—Mrs. Taylor (finally stops playing the djembe) runs over
—Mrs. T: "Girls, what is going on here? Have some compassion for each other, please."

> –me: "Fuck compassion. Remember 'Respect the Experience?' Well I'm feeling my experience."
>
> –Thought that—didn't say.
>
> –What I did say: "Lily is calling me a 'nigger.'"

She looks at Lilly and she says, "Lilly, How Dare You." So Lilly says, "But she was calling me a nigger." And then Ms. Taylor looks at me and says, "Well now, Lilly can't be a nigger."

William film

Baldwin text 4 in response to Nigger Story (after William film)
Well, respect for the experience is a kind of compassion, even though I may want to blow your head off. I have to know both things at once. One has to accept this field of proposition; everything that's been done, however horrible, if it was done by another human being, it could be done by me. Who knows where one could be driven?

Drummer film

Keyword solos/Rapture/Orb/Onion

No Room Story

Do you remember Elias, Jeff's grandson? Wasn't it his birthday? That day Jeff and Jenny got all dressed up like they were going to a wedding? I know they didn't forget Elias's birthday. But where was he?

"That boy didn't even wait to say goodbye . . ."

I know he was the one who picked up the plate pieces, again, and yes, he was humiliated, at least embarrassed. He picked them up anyway, being careful not to cut his hands . . . later he ran off . . .

Jeff was inside, turning off the light. Preparing to be lost in the one last thing he had to do before he could leave. There he is. Who, Elias? No, Jeff. Where? There, in the other room. He's talking. I think he's talking to himself.

"Dere is nothin' happens by chance, without you 'spectin' it. All dere is, is de strength, de power, de vigor of what you don' know."

A phrase he'd learned from William, sweet William, a long time ago. He has said this before, every time . . . He doesn't acknowledge that this may be the last time, but maybe he does. This is going to be the last time. Right, Jeff? The last time. His long fingers tricking with sleight-of-hand, inside his half-propped-up pants, between his legs. His power, his control. He even took off his shirt this time, the one he had so painstakingly just put on.

Until he knocks his head softly back against the wall where there is sound, a little howl, and then tears, waking him momentarily. The room stays put, has not commented. The little light coming from the window has not shifted.

His head and folded body now rest against the gray pitch of the wall and floor. He's thinking again. "Nah. Nah, I ain't scairt. Dere is nothin' happens by chance, without you 'spectin' it, ever." Eyes closed, lips reflecting little signs of recovery. Come on, Jeff. You have five more minutes and then you have to walk out the door. "Now where is my damn shirt?"

"I's almost ready, Jennie." I can hardly hear him. "I loves you mo' than you'll ever know."

Down the slope to the right of Jeff's house were cultivated acres. A tiny thread of a road ran through these green fields like a pencil mark. At the farthest end of this mark was a dot. Elias, spinning . . . hopping . . . running around in a big old circle over and over again. I know what Jennie's thinking. She's thinking, "That boy's goin' to get into trouble . . ."

RL Solo #2 w/ Darrell clock

SNT 1 w/ Baldwin text 5
I thought to myself, if I do this he'll jump there. If he jumps there and I do this, he'll go there. And if I make my next move, if he jumps here, then I got him. And it always worked.

Blood Sweat and Tears song: "I love you more than you'll ever know."

DD has first spin, in silence

SNT 2

Okwui sings the Smiths, "Please, Please, Please Let Me Get What I Want" during DD's second spin.

Darrell has cross-over solo

Gesel and David have retro duet

Sex story/ Girl at fountain/Verdi's *Otello*/Attic Agreement

Sex Story Outline

David: So, how old were you?

Okwui: [sixteen . . .]

—watching him, next door, shooting hoops in the driveway

David: Was it summer?

Okwui: [yes . . .]

—decision to do it—picked his birthday

—told my parents X

—met at Kelly Ingram Park at fountain, waiting, beers
—he shows up with a tie

—attic—rejection (with 2-part underpant/pant combo and lights on/off)—humilation, bed

—breakfast, back to attic—"What do you want to do" exchange

—"You can't stop me" deal

—now we're doing it
        –tongue travels—teaching words in different languages
        [–broad back—marking]
        –disappearing—turning into a dot—changing

(when Okwui feels it beginning to hit an end, she lets it trail off, float, and continues thinking about it without words)

David: [after a pause] Was there a wedding?

Okwui: No, there was no wedding . . .

"Ne me quitte pas" dance (trio) w/Okwui and DD playing (Naumaning) w/horseshoes and basketball hoop/Picnic film

Horse Story/Okwui/Duluth film

He ran around in that circle for the longest time, and then something happened. A few minutes later I was at the window, my voice rattling against the pane like a broken shutter.

"I'm ready, Jeff."

He didn't answer, was buttoning his shirt. He limped out of the house hitching up his tie. Standing outside the door he took a deep breath, smelling the air, and surveyed our green fields. Then he led me across the yard toward the shed. After a few steps a quick shudder passed over him, and he froze. Jesus!

"How come you shaking so?" I whispered.
"I don't know, Jennie."
"You must be scairt, Jeff."
"No, baby, I ain't scairt. I just was wonderin' about Elias and all of a sudden remembered John . . . that young man I knew when I was a chap."
"Why you thinkin' 'bout that now?' I squeezed his hand. "Come on, Jeff, don't be just standin' there, we gotta get that old horse ready."
"Oh, yes, right away, baby . . . just give me a minute . . . I was just turnin' things round in ma mind . . ."

(sitting in memory space)

He was goin' with Miss Lilly Wallace, John was. Her husband was dead. Miss Taylor, her sister, stayed with her that night, saw John sneakin' out Lilly's window and turned him in. Because of the rain they tracked him. Brought him over to the sheriff's place. The sheriff promised John if he told him the truth he wouldn't let them get 'im. John told the truth and the sheriff hollered, "Come and get 'im boys!" John was stupid, believin' the sheriff like that, "Come and get 'im boys!" Well, they got him. That's the way it always worked.

(pause)

It was a big o' plum tree. We called it 'gator limb, us chilluns, played up under it everyday. That's why they hung him there I bet.

David asks: Is the tree still there, the plum tree?

226

Okwui. Oh man, no! No, man, no! That was a long time ago. Now it's a street light, a yellow pole.

Duluth text 2/RL (in attic)/Duluth film
"Elias got into trouble . . .that summer visiting his Aunt Tempy up north, Jennie's sister, in Duluth.
Creating rituals, improvisational-memorials throughout the state, places where something bad happened. He was so serious.
"This is an act of sympathy," that's what he told the police officer, quoting James Baldwin. It was a really interesting idea. But all fake finally. He would suspend his body from specifically chosen vertical objects. Hanging/falling in space, not up, not down, or falling up and down, from streetlights, bridges, trees, there were lots of trees. Once from an open fire hydrant . . . there was not much falling distance but he did get really really wet. But not here, here it was a yellow streetlight pole . . . and a few memories; one was of all that water.

It began the day that Jeff and Jennie got all dressed up, walked out their house to the shed, and rode their scrawny little horse off a cliff together. They fell, holding on to each other tightly, showing no excitement, the water booming below.

Elias was a young boy then, was there, watching from the top of the hill [Walking Table on], thinking it was all his fault. It wasn't.
The horse was the first to hit the water . . . then Jeff . . . Jennie . . .
[horse first move]
Damn, they aren't even scared.
[horse second move]
Oh shit, they weren't scared at all.

Elias got older, was much older when he stood next to that yellow pole. He was arrested that summer in Duluth on his birthday. Spent a few days in the county jail . . . when he got home, he made this dance.

Hose dance/RL
Mississippi/end Duluth
Ecstasy
Ecstasy re-dux

Baldwin text 6 edited
"It involves another sense, one more difficult to articulate. But that sense has something to do with the presence of Africa. Even though it's a very unreadable presence, it's a real one. Real in a way it was not for me when I was young and old. Or even as it was not real, let's say, fifteen, twenty years ago.
Something is beginning to happen in the Western world and everybody, in one way or another, is feeling this. In short, the center, that presumed to be the center of the earth has shifted, and the definition of man has shifted with it."

Does that make sense to you?

p. 32
Swedish manufacturer Ikea opened its first North American manufacturing center in Danville in 2008. By 2011 Ikea was the target of racial discrimination complaints, a heated union-organizing battle, and turnover from disgruntled employees.

p. 61
C: Please state your name and age.
R: Who will you show this to?

I wrote the questions I wanted to ask my father on a discount, travel-sized memo pad before we left New York. Skipping lines, I made room to jot in his answers.

REPORT FROM VIRGINIA IN 1961:
RICHMOND: 'COLORED' SIGNS NEWLY REMOVED FROM THE STATION.
DANVILLE: FIRST FREEDOM RIDER REFUSED SERVICE.

C: What comes to mind when you think of the American South?
R: Dust.

REPORT FROM NORTH CAROLINA IN 1961:
GREENSBORO: BLACKS ONLY WAITING ROOM RECENTLY CLOSED.
CHARLOTTE: FIRST FREEDOM RIDER ARRESTED FOR SITTING AT A SHOESHINE STAND AFTER BEING REFUSED SERVICE.

C: What's your earliest memory of racial inequality or prejudice?
R: My brother remembers a story that I don't remember of the two of us in an apartment complex playground where a little white boy ran up to us and called us Niggers. That was the first time my brother remembers being called a Nigger. And I don't remember the story at all.

REPORT FROM SOUTH CAROLINA IN 1961:
ROCKHILL: FREEDOM RIDERS FIRST ATTACKED BY A GROUP OF YOUNG WHITE MEN.

C: What's your favorite family legend?
R: The story of my grandfather, my mother's father. He would drink a lot and one day he drank too much and got the heebie geebies—which is you see things that aren't there. He got the heebie geebies and ran through the woods looking at green elephants. Not sure this never happened.

REPORT FROM GEORGIA IN 1961:
TWO NIGHTS AND ONE DAY OF REST.
MARTIN LUTHOR KING JR. TOOK THE FREEDOM RIDERS OUT TO DINNER.

C: Did you ever personally experience segregation on a bus?
R: No. Yes. When I was 5 or 6 or 7, my mother and my brother and I were going to Lancaster, South Carolina from Ohio and I recall sitting on the back of the bus. It was really crowded in the back, and I actually remember sleeping on the floor under my mother's feet.

REPORT FROM ALABAMA IN 1961:
ANNISTON: THE FREEDOM RIDERS ARE FIREBOMBED.
BIRMINGHAM: AFTER A VIOLENT ATTACK BY THE KU KLUX KLAN, THE ORIGINAL FREEDOM RIDERS ARE REPLACED BY THE STUDENT NONVIOLENT COORDINATING COMMITTEE. (SNCC)
MONTGOMERY: SNCC ARE SURROUNDED AT THE BUS STATION, MARTIN LUTHER KING JR. ASKED THAT THEY STOP THE RIDES FOR A COOLING OFF PERIOD. JAMES FARMER RESPONDED; "WE'VE BEEN COOLING OFF FOR THREE HUNDRED AND FIFTY YEARS. IF WE COOL OFF ANY MORE, WE'LL BE IN A DEEP FREEZE."

C: What do you love most about black people?
R: Our vulnerability.

REPORT FROM MISSISSIPPI IN 1961:
JACKSON: THE RIDERS ARE ARRESTED AND SENTENCED TO THE STATE PENITENTIARY. THEY WOULD GO NO FARTHER.

C. If there was one thing your mother always said, what was it?
R. My mother always said that I should come home. That's what she always said, Come home.

p. 90
The first 45 record I ever bought, 1966, was "96 Tears," by Question Mark and the Mysterians. The flip side was "Midnight Hour." The lead singer, ?, claimed to be a Martian.

p. 133
A few years later (2006?) Walter made a few corrections to my earlier fieldtrip notes: that "Gary" was actually "Jerry" and that "Gator Limb," the tree where they hung Gary, I mean Jerry, is actually "Jerry's Limb." I learn that the uncle who blew his brains out after seeing "the big black buzzard-like bird, a prophesy bird" actually saw a "big blue cock bird," which may also be a "prophesy bird," and then had his brains "blown out" by someone else. It was not a suicide.
"It was late at night, in the dark. He had just finished workin' in the field, on his way home. He was a rough 'un anyway, so who knows," Walter reminisced.
And I learned, with some karmic appreciation, that Captain Taylor, the sheriff behind Jerry's lynching, a long time ago, eventually killed himself, committed suicide.

p. 140
In 2010 it was revealed that, from at least 1968 until 1970, Withers was a prolific FBI informant who passed on tips and photographs detailing an insider's view of politics, business, and everyday life in Memphis's black community. Withers shadowed King the day before his murder, snapping photos and telling agents about a meeting the civil rights leader had with suspected black militants.
Much of his undercover work helped the FBI break up the Invaders, a Black Panther–styled militant group that became popular in disaffected black Memphis in the late 1960s and was feared by city leaders.

p. 159
In October 2003, the Clayton Jackson McGhie Memorial was commemorated, a memorial plaza built across the street from the site of the lynching, the largest lynching monument in the U.S.

p. 208
May 3, 2011. Was walking home today, to my apartment in the East Village and passed a young brown boy, maybe 8 or 9 years old, walking very animatedly alone. He almost seemed to be dancing, quirky, agitated and held, displayed a copy of the New York Times. As he passed me he poked his finger at the front page, the big photograph of Osama Bin Laden, and blurted, "He's dead, they killed him, killed him, yay!! He's dead!" And then he punched the front page, dropped the paper a little lower to his body and kicked it, twice, the photograph, Osama Bin Laden's bearded, turbaned, and smiling portrait.

How old are you, I asked?

"10."

You're awfully pissed off at that guy!

"Yeah, he bombed the Twin Towers! I hate him! He's dead!"

He sprightly hopped away, continuing to battle with (or caress) his copy of the Times, poking, punching, kicking, exhilarated. He's dead, he's dead!

(And I wondered where he got a copy of the New York Times, this child. I doubt he bought it, or had a subscription.)

I give special thanks to my family and friends from the South for the many Southern stories: Ralph and Ruth Lemon, Mike Lemon, Mattie Belk, William Funderburk, Joan Lemon, Lawrence Guyot, Rosalinda McGloin, Otha Turner, Hicks Walker, Cornelia Bailey, and the Hog Hammock community of Sapelo Island, GA, Jimmy "Duck" Holmes, and the Blue Front Cafe, Buddy Spires, Mr. Walter and Edna Carter, Clementine Davis, Helen Kent, Jessie Mae Hemphill, Ruby Brown, the girl at the fountain, the drummer at Otha Turner's picnic, the dancers at Otha Turner's picnic, Mrs. Mitchell, Mae Smith, Mose T.

And to David Thomson, Darrell Jones, Djédjé Djédjé Gervais, Gesel Mason Okwui Okpokwasili, Katherine Profeta, and all those who helped in the physical and structural processes along the way: Nari Ward, R. Eric Stone, Roderick Murray, Christian Marclay, Lucas Indelicato, Mike Taylor, Anne C. de Velder, Douglas Repetto, F. Randy deCelle, Eric Petajan, Cori Haveson, James Hanaham, Bebe Miller, Miko Doi Smith, Goulei Tchépoho, and Angelo Kouakou Yao.

I'd like to thank MAPP, now and before; Ann Rosenthal, Cathy Zimmerman, Jordana Phokompe, Joyce Lawler, Lisa Phillips, Liz Filbrun, Emily Harney, Michelle Coe, and Arnie Zimmerman for holding this process up after the many times it seemed it would fall apart, especially Ann, who endured this precariousness for nine years.

To those who provided research space and resources: African American Cultural Center, Pittsburgh, PA; Atlantic Center for the Arts, New Smyrna Beach, FL; Blue Front Cafe, Bentonia, MS; Brooklyn Academy of Music, The Kitchen and Outpost Video, NYC; House of World Cultures, Berlin; Institute for Studies in the Arts and the Public Events Program at Arizona State University, Tempe; Krannert Center for the Performing Arts at the University of Illinois, Urbana–Champaign; Museum of Contemporary Art, Chicago; Oakes African American Cultural Center, Yazoo City, MS; Princeton University, NJ; the Rockefeller Foundation's Bellagio Center; SICARS cultural organization, Sapelo Island, GA; UCLA Department of World Arts & Culture, CA; Virginia Commonwealth University, Richmond; Walker Art Center, Minneapolis; Wesleyan Center for the Arts, Middletown, CT.

I thank Wayne Ashley, John Mitchell, Patricia Clark, Siew Kong Wong, Hari Sundaram, John Klima, Thanassis Rikakis, and Steve Dietz for helping translate the research from an electronic-online point of view, dismantling the standard hierarchy.

Bruce Langhorne for the folk music lesson. MMK for the original "No Room" story. My very patient board: Elissa Bernstein, Jack Kupferman, Norton Owen, Baraka Sele, and Stanley Smith.

Supporters and friends, Sam Miller, Cynthia Mayeda, Philip Bither, Joe Melillo, Neil Barclay, Jennifer Goodale, and Colleen Jennings-Roggensack.

Heartfelt thanks to Chelsea Lemon-Fetzer for her enduring partnership. To Asako Takami for the gift of Ukiyo. And to Jimena Paz for right now.

There are many more to thank, and unfortunately I've run out of room to do it here. But I want to thank Stan Wojewodski Jr. and Mike Ross for the beginning, the middle, and the beginning.

And to Suzanna Tamminen and Wesleyan University Press for taking this writing seriously, Jenn Joy and Bronwyn Becker for the helpful editing. And Rina Root for making it a real book.

About the Author

Ralph Lemon is Artistic Director of Cross Performance, a company dedicated to the creation of cross-cultural and cross-disciplinary performance and presentation. Lemon builds teams of collaborating artists from diverse cultural backgrounds, countries, and artistic disciplines who bring their own history and aesthetic voices to the work. Projects develop over a period of years, with public sharings of work-in-progress, culminating in artworks derived from the artistic, cultural, historical, and emotional material uncovered in this rigorous creative research process.

In 2005 Lemon concluded *The Geography Trilogy*, a decade-long international research and performance project exploring the "conceptual materials" of race, history, memory, and the creative practice. The project featured three dance/theater performances: *Geography* (1997), *Tree* (2000), and *Come home Charley Patton* (2004). In addition, it included two Internet art projects, several gallery exhibitions, and the publication of three books by Wesleyan University Press, of which this is the third. Other recent projects include the three-DVD set of *The Geography Trilogy*; a web installation (www.ralphlemon.net); a 2009 multimedia performance commission for the Lyon Opera Ballet, *Rescuing the Princess*; and a current multimedia project, *How Can You Stay in the House All Day and Not Go Anywhere?*

Lemon was one of fifty artists to receive the inaugural United States Artists Fellowship in 2006. He has received two "Bessie" (New York Dance and Performance) Awards, a 2004 New York Foundation for the Arts Prize for Choreography, a Guggenheim Fellowship, and a 2004 Fellowship with the Bellagio Study and Conference Center. In 1999 Lemon was honored with the CalArts Alpert Award in the Arts. Lemon has been artist-in-residence at Temple University in Philadelphia (2005–6), George A. Miller Endowment Visiting Artist at the Krannert Center (2004), and a Fellow of the Humanities Council and Program in Theater and Dance at Princeton University (2002). From 1996 to 2000 he was associate artist at Yale Repertory Theatre. Most recently he was an IDA Fellow at Stanford University. He is currently a visiting critic at the Yale School of Art, Sculpture Department.

Lemon's solo visual art exhibitions include *How Can You Stay in the House All Day and Not Go Anywhere?* (Yerba Buena Center for the Arts, San Francisco, 2010); *(the efflorescence of) Walter* (Contemporary Art Center, New Orleans, 2008; The Kitchen, New York, 2007; and Walker Art Center, Minneapolis, 2006); *The Geography Trilogy* (Zilkha Gallery at Wesleyan University, Middletown, CT, 2001); *Temples* (Margaret Bodell Gallery, New York, 2000); and *Geography* (Art Awareness, Lexington, NY, 1997). Group exhibitions include *Move: Choreographing You* (Hayward Gallery, London, 2010–11) and *The Record: Contemporary Art and Vinyl* (Nasher Museum at Duke University, Durham, NC). In January 2011 Lemon performed at the Museum of Modern Art in New York City in conjunction with the exhibition *On Line: Drawing Through the Twentieth Century.*